What the reviewers say:

Highly recommended by leaders in pastoral counseling: A timely book. Dr. Hulme has focused the concerns of pastoral counseling at the heart of what being a pastor is all about.

Wayne E. Oates, University of Louisville

A balanced text showing the need for pastors to acquire psychological skill and depth in their own theological disciplines.

Paul W. Pruyser, Menninger Foundation

A unique perception of pastoral ministry comes alive in this book.

Edgar N. Jackson

Argues effectively that prayer, Bible, meditation, sacraments, and talk about God have a place in pastoral care and counseling.

Seward Hiltner, Princeton Seminary

An excellent book on biblically-oriented pastoral counseling.

Granger E. Westberg, Chicago

Hulme demonstrates that it is possible to homogenize classical theology with modern psychotherapeutic principles.

Orlo Strunk, editor, The Journal of Pastoral Care

Constructive suggestions on how to integrate effective caring with the expression of the Gospel.

David K. Switzer, Southern Methodist University

This is a book that will help pastoral counselors integrate biblical and theological resources with their counseling and pastoral care in ways that are enablers of spiritual growth.

Howard Clinebell, School of Theology at Claremont

Hulme challenges both those who are superficial to gain depth and understanding, and those who forsake pastoral identity to be pastors with religious symbols. A book for clergy and seminarians who want to be the "aroma of Christ" and not "peddlers of the Gospel."

Edward J. Mahnke, Texas Medical Center

Opens fresh insights into the place of scripture, meditation and prayer in pastoral counseling, while avoiding their often stereotyped use as tools.

John R. Thomas

William E. Hulme

Using the Unique
Resources of
the Christian
Tradition

PASTORAL CARE & COUNSELING

AUGSBURG Publishing House • Minneapolis

PASTORAL CARE AND COUNSELING

Copyright © 1981 Augsburg Publishing House

Library of Congress Catalog Card No. 80-67806

International Standard Book No. 0-8066-1869-8

Scripture quotations unless otherwise noted are from the Revised Standard Version of the Bible, copyright 1946, 1952, and 1971 by the Division of Christian Education of the National Council of Churches.

MANUFACTURED IN THE UNITED STATES OF AMERICA

Contents

1

Uniquely Pastoral Resources

My purpose in this book is not to teach the fundamentals of counseling or even of pastoral care and counseling. There are books available in this area, and I see no need for another. The basic approach of listening to feelings, although new to pastoral education a few decades ago, is now common knowledge, even if not common practice. In addition to the changes that have taken place in pastoral education in theological seminaries, the clinical pastoral education movement for four decades has been supervising pastors and theological students in pastoral care and counseling, primarily within medical and correctional institutional settings. The contributions of secular psychotherapists such as Carl Rogers, and later Eric Berne and Fritz Perls and others, have all played their role in this education, as the words "non-directive" (later "client-centered"), "transactional analysis" (TA) and "Gestalt" have become part of the growing movement to equip the clergy to minister effectively to their "hurting" parishioners.

Critics of Pastoral Care and Counseling

This movement has not been without critics both from within and without. During the 1950s I wrote an article for the *Christian Century* attempting to correlate the emerging pastoral insights with theology. My opening sentence was "Pastoral counseling as it is now understood attempts to incorporate the teachings of the psychology of personality into the techniques of the clinical psychologist into the ministry of religion." The *Century* editor inserted "currently something of a fad," as a descriptive phrase following the words, "pastoral counseling."

Since then there have been many subsequent "fads" that have occupied the focus of theological and clergy concerns. Now that pastoral counseling has "come of age," however, some have accused it of departing from its ministerial roots. Not only has pastoral counseling incorporated much from the psychological disciplines, it has, according to this criticism, *become* a psychological discipline. The theology that may be obvious in worship seems absent in pastoral counseling. Rather than integrating psychological insights into the ministry of counseling, say these critics, pastoral counseling has divorced itself from its traditional religious base. If pastoral counselors have become more psychologists or psychotherapists than pastors, then pastoral counseling has lost its uniqueness or even distinctiveness.

This criticism of pastoral counseling may be unfair, particularly when it is made by those who do not recognize something as pastoral unless it is accompanied by traditional verbal or ritual symbols, and who do not recognize the difference between pastoral care and pastoral counseling. The essence of any ministry should not become synonymous with the customary symbols used in its performance.

On the other hand, there may be truth to the criticism, coming as it has from those also who are *insiders* (such as Don Browning and Thomas Oden)—who are themselves knowledgeable in the discipline. As one becomes proficient in the use of counseling skills, a psychological base can subtly replace a theological one. Some pastoral counselors who are sensitive to this criticism have attempted to counter it by showing religious parallels to what they are doing or by adding religious words or acts to their counseling.

While these efforts are helpful in showing the relationship of religion to their counseling discipline, they are not essentially what is meant by a theological integration. Such integration takes place initially within the person of the counselors, which in turn leads counselors to express this integration in their counseling. On the other hand, as counselors follow a structure which manifests this integration, they are reenforcing their own internal integration.

Differentiation Between Pastoral Care and Counseling

Since this is a book on pastoral care and counseling, we need to define these terms and to distinguish between them. *Pastoral care* is a supportive ministry to people and those close to them who are experiencing the familiar trials that characterize life in this world, such as illness, surgery, incapacitation, death, and bereavement. The Book of Job describes the purpose of the visit of the three friends to the stricken Job in pastoral-care terms: "They made an appointment together to come to condole with him and comfort him" (2:11). The pastor's hospital ministry is a specific example of pastoral care. On the other hand, *pastoral counseling,* either in one-to-one relationships or in groups, is a ministry to persons, couples, and families that assists them in working through pressing problems in their relationship to themselves, to others, and to God. Both are dialogical ministries, and both are oriented to the healing process in pain and suffering.

They are distinguished in these respects from preaching, administering the sacraments, pastoral administration, teaching, and other nurturing ministries. Obviously the purpose of both pastoral care and counseling is related to these other ministries, and they are interrelated in their influence upon people.

These other ministries are also implicitly and sometimes explicitly dialogical. The differentiation is a matter of emphasis. So the overlapping is obvious. For example, premarital guidance is basically an educational ministry. Yet, depending on how dialogically it is conducted, it may also lead to issues that could involve pastoral counseling. The interrelationship and overlapping of these ministries are most clearly apparent when all of the ministries of the congregation constitute a resource for pastoral care and counseling, as we will see in the last chapter of this book.

This same overlapping is true also between pastoral care and counseling. A hospitalized parishioner, for example, in receiving pastoral care, may reveal that she is anxious and suspicious over the infrequent visits of her spouse; the need then is disclosed for pastoral counseling in a marriage problem. Psychosomatic overtures also may be apparent with specific persons who are ill, and the pastor may need to combine his or her pastoral care with pastoral counseling to deal with these. In his or her pastoral care of a bereaved spouse, the pastor may perceive in the inconsolableness of acute grief, an unresolved guilt over one's relationship with the deceased. This constitutes an obstacle to healthy grieving. In order to remove this obstacle, the pastor may need to shift to the medium of pastoral counseling.

By the same token, a pastoral-counseling ministry may move into pastoral care. After the obstacle of guilt has been worked through in the above instance, for example, the pastor will still need to give pastoral care to this person for a year or more following the death. In a death of this nature the grieving process usually takes at least this long.

Because of the close association of the two activities, the title for the course in pastoral counseling at the seminary where I teach has been changed to *Basic Principles of Pastoral Care and Counseling,* since the students spend part of their clinical experience for the course in a general hospital and the other in more counseling-oriented opportunities, such as drug-dependency treatment-centers and correctional facilities.

All those who function as pastors, either in the parish or as institutional chaplains, are involved in both pastoral care and counseling interchangeably. While we need to distinguish between the two, it would be extremely difficult to separate them in the pastoral ministry. The only exception would be for those clergy in private practice as pastoral counselors, and perhaps also those who function as staff persons in medical or mental-health clinics. By virtue of the context within which they minister, these persons are confined to pastoral counseling.

Whether the criticism of pastoral counseling is fair or unfair in any particular instance, it must not becloud the fact that pastoral counseling is a unique form of counseling. My purpose in this book is to focus on this uniqueness. I shall assume a general knowledge of counseling on the part of the reader and will refer to this knowledge in my description of the theology that underlies it and of the religious resources used in conjunction with it.

Focusing in the Uniqueness

The Clinical Pastoral Education movement has succeeded to a large extent in exposing the superficial use of the traditional religious resources in pastoral care. Prayer, for example, has been exploited as a way of escaping from the demands of serious dialogue. Pastors misusing prayer in this way often reflect their evasiveness also in the *way* they pray. Instead of being specific in their petitions concerning their counselee's needs, they resort to the generalities of familiar prayer cliches. Religious words have also been misused to stifle dialogue. Rather than deal directly with a counselee's resistance, pastors may seek to suppress it by taking on the authority role in religion. Retreating to the protected sphere associated with preaching, they use "God-talk"—religiously oriented words associated with the profession—as an attempt to maintain control of the situation. Genuine dialogue, on the other hand, requires the relinquishment of this control, and the dialoguer risks an unpredictable outcome in each encounter.

While pastoral counseling, particularly in its clinical pastoral education dimension, has been very effective in exposing these defensive uses of traditional religious resources, it has not been so successful in developing a discipline or structure for an appropriate or effective use of these resources. It is to this task that I am directing myself. My purpose is to provide a text in pastoral care and counseling which shows the use of these distinctively religious resources that stem from the theological and ecclesiastical base of the discipline.

The reaction of my graduate students to my suggestion that we spend some time on the use of "God-talk" in pastoral counseling was typical. They expressed apprehension. Having been emancipated from a pastoral compulsion to use God-talk through their clinical pastoral education, they were concerned about any kind of return to it. God-talk in counseling had become synonymous with superficiality. The resource had been so poorly used that they doubted the possibility of its effective use.

This reaction is quite understandable in the light of our pastoral history. It takes a while for the effects of misuse to be placed in a broader perspective. Hopefully that time has come. The ultimate response to misuse is not disuse, but proper use. It took a leap of faith on the part of these students to believe there *was* a proper use. Yet their hesitance was also an advantage: they had the needed caution to use the resources with care.

The first decision a pastoral counselor must make regarding his or her religious resources is when to use them—and when to abstain. The next decision is actually more than a decision, although it is phrased as such. *How* does one use these resources when the context is deemed appropriate? What is their *counseling* use, as differentiated from a *teaching* or a *preaching* use? What are the criteria that assist the pastor to know why

and when and how to use these resources? Although the answers to these questions naturally depend upon the development of a skill or the proficiency of an art, we will attempt to
deal with them in this book.

The Symbolic Role of Pastor

The uniqueness of pastoral care and counseling is focused on
the meaning of the word *pastoral*. The title *pastor* carries a
symbolic role with a long tradition. My students often struggle
with this authority role. Some are inhibited by it, feeling no
longer free to be themselves. Others find it a boost to their personal confidence and may prefer wearing a clerical collar to
fortify this confidence. I see my task as assisting them to perceive their symbol-bearing function as an asset to the counselee.
Because they are pastors, they can minister with an authority
that can liberate people from the religious legalisms, distorted
pieties, and secular limitations that imprison them. The pastor
is an ordained minister of the church, vested with leadership
in the community of faith. Although lay as well as clergy may
perform pastoral acts, the symbolic role centers in the ordination by the church of specific pastors charged with responsibility for the nurture of a worshiping and witnessing body of
believers. The language associated with this community is, as
we have indicated, commonly called God-talk, an indication of
the transcendent dimension of the community's faith. This language contains the words of Good News since it tells the story
of God's coming through Christ into our alienated and fallen
existence and of his victory in Christ over the forces of destruction and death.

The means for receiving the Good News are traditionally
described as Word and sacraments. The Word is the verbal
symbol of communication associated primarily with the Bible,
while the sacraments (or *rites* as some groups call them) are
primarily the non-verbal symbols of communication of the

rites and rituals of the community: namely the *washing* of Baptism and the *eating* and *drinking* of the Lord's Supper. Some communities of faith give greater emphasis to the Word, others emphasize the sacraments, and still others attempt to hold each in balance. These differences among the communities of faith are similar to the differences among families regarding the roles played by verbal and non-verbal communication. Both of these—Word and sacrament—are specific religious resources in pastoral counseling.

The response of the community to God's overture of love in Christ is to engage in a dialogue of intimacy that is commonly defined as prayer and meditation. Participation in the Lord's Supper is itself an act of worship. The community's response is also diffused into the world in ministry to people. While each believer is personally called by God to this service, this sense of vocation is sustained by the community. Each of these —prayer and meditation, vocation under God and the practice of community—is a specific religious resource in pastoral care and counseling.

Structure of This Book

The structure of this book reflects this description of the tradition that identifies the word *pastoral.* We begin with a functional description of the Christian faith in its particular references to the ministry of pastoral care and counseling. This is *pastoral* theology—the unique perspective by which one views life as a Christian. The next two chapters are specific developments of this theology in its character of Good News. Chapter 2 is a pastoral development of the theology of reconciliation for the alienated state of fallen humanity—the Good News of forgiveness and restoration to intimacy as a positive resolution to the bondage of sin and guilt. In Chapter 3 our focus is on the relationship of this specific faith to the universal experience of death. It is the Good News also of the affirmation of victory over death—with all of its symbols and symptoms—through the resurrection of Christ. The pastoral office, obviously, is uniquely equipped to minister in this experience of ultimate loss, both to the dying and to the bereaved, since its symbolic role is heavily identified with the hope of eternal life. These three chapters form a cognitive base for which the religious resources of pastoral care and counseling described in the following chapters are functional expressions.

Chapter 4 is a direct application of this specific faith of the pastor to the dialogical process of pastoral care and counseling. The focus here is on the language of faith—God-talk—as it relates to the pastoral dialogue. It is through the interpersonal dynamics of dialogue that the specific faith is verbally communicated in pastoral counseling. In Chapter 5 the subject is the use of the Bible—the written deposit of the Good News—as a religious resource in pastoral care and counseling. This chapter concludes with a description of meditation as one of the ways in which the pastor can utilize this Word of God in his or her pastoral ministry. We move in Chapter 6 to the human response to the Word, namely prayer. Prayer's use in pastoral care and counseling is in line with the catalyzing and supportive purposes of these ministries. Principles and guidelines are offered for when and how to utilize prayer for these purposes. In the final chapter we shall concentrate on the community of faith itself, the congregation or parish, together with its sacrament of Holy Communion. This community is organically related to the pastoral office, and the sacrament is a celebrative means of receiving from God. Both are valuable resources in pastoral care and counseling. The therapy inherent in the worship, vocational, and fellowship aspects of this community provides a unique support group for people in their common confrontation with life's inevitable stresses.

2

The Specific Faith
of Pastoral Care
and Counseling

When I am referred to as a teacher of counseling in a theological seminary, I accept it if my time is limited. If there is time, however, I correct it: "Not counseling, rather *pastoral* counseling." Some appreciate the clarification; others ask—some honestly, others sarcastically—"Is there a difference?"

Pastoral counseling is a form of counseling, but a *specific* form. As such it is unique among its fellow disciplines. Our concern in this chapter is what constitutes its uniqueness, and because of this uniqueness, its organic relationship to pastoral care.

In-Commonness

Before we discuss pastoral counseling's uniqueness, we need to examine what it has in common with other forms of counseling. Pastoral counseling has received much from the various schools of psychotherapy; in fact, so much that pastoral counselors may lose sight of their distinctive identity. Paul Pruyser, for example, believes that pastoral counselors are so influenced by the psychologically-oriented counselors that they diagnose their counselee's disturbances by psychological concepts rather than by those native to their own discipline. Pruyser himself is a clinical psychologist who has worked closely with pastors, particularly those involved in clinical pastoral education. His observation corresponds with my own: that when pastoral counselors function primarily with psychological rather than theological concepts, they are not only failing those who seek their help for religious reasons, but they are also failing to fulfill their complementary role in a teamwork approach with other members of the helping professions.

Pastoral counseling has much in common with other forms of counseling. The dynamics of dialogue that constitute counseling are shared by all. Human nature and human interactions do not change because of the kind of counseling involved. For this reason counselors can learn much from each other, even though they differ in the perspective within which they counsel. Pastoral counselors, for example, may use concepts and techniques from Transactional Analysis, Gestalt, Rational-Emotive, or Client-Centered Therapy and yet function within their own unique perspective.

All forms of counseling share common assumptions which are essentially common articles of faith. Article One is the faith that each discipline has in its own approach, perspective, and techniques. The counselor's own confidence in his or her way of functioning is important for the counselee's confidence as well. This faith need not discount the worth and effectiveness of other forms of counseling. It is simply an ease with one's own way of doing things. Should this faith be undermined by doubt, one would be seriously looking into other options.

Article Two is faith in the healing power of a relationship. Carl Rogers, founder of Client-Centered Therapy, in subjecting his approach to testing procedures, concluded that attitudes were more decisive than technique in the process of therapy. Three of these attitudes are needed in the counselor. The first is congruence—being the same person on the inside as on the outside. Congruence would preclude manipulative techniques in which the counselor's real purpose remains hidden. The second is an empathic identification with the inner world of the counselee *as if* it were one's own. (The words, *as if,* are important since it is *not* his own.) The third is an unconditionally positive regard for the counselee. This attitude corresponds to the biblical description of love as *agape.* The fourth of these attitudes belongs to the counselee, since a dialogue is determined not only by one of its participants, but by both. Consequently there needs to be at least a minimal response to these qualities of the counselor on the part of the counselee. Persons with pronounced sociopathic tendencies, for example, find it difficult to respond to a counseling relationship because they project their long and painful history of rejection and distrust onto the counselor. In assuming he has an "angle" as they do, they often fail to contribute honestly to the dialogue.

While Article Two may seem to be more one of fact than of faith to some, in our computer- and chemically-oriented age we seem to question the efficiency of anything as time-consuming and subjective as therapy through relationship. In fact, some forms of behavior modification may have only a small portion of their faith invested in the therapist-client relationship. Yet even in these instances the relationship between therapist and client establishes the rapport that supports the motivating influences for change.

The Third Article of faith is faith in a process of personal growth or change that is inherent in human nature. This process, of course, needs to be abetted by appropriate conditions. Each school of psychotherapy sees its own approach as a catalyst in the activating of this inherent potential for growth. As stated by Virginia Satir, "We cannot create human life, we can only activate it."

The uniqueness of pastoral counseling is in a specific faith that includes but also transcends this common faith. This is a faith not only of the pastoral counselor but also of the particular tradition he or she represents and the worshiping community of which he or she is pastor. Though this specific faith is not always articulated in a counseling session, it is implicit in a way similar to the common faith. Although counseling may and often does include education, it is not primarily education in the precise sense of the term. Whether or not the specific faith is made explicit in the session is determined by the context of the moment, the openness of the dialogue to it. Either way, whether implicit or explicit, the specific faith is basic to *pastoral* counseling.

The purpose of counseling is to facilitate change in the life of the person seeking it. The specific faith of pastoral counseling is basic because it is a power to effect change. My purpose in this chapter is to describe this faith at its functional dimension—in other words, from the perspective of pastoral theology. In its distinction from systematic, historical and exegetical (biblical) theology, pastoral theology is the body of knowledge that has resulted from reflection on the revelation of God in Christ as it relates to the intra-personal, inter-personal, and group dynamics of human functioning. As such it is the cognitive material from which the ministries of pastoral care and counseling take their shape. Reflection on these ministries in the light of this revelation, in turn, adds to the evolving knowledge of pastoral theology. (Seward Hiltner provides a thorough development of the distinction of pastoral theology as differentiated from other branches of theology in *Preface to Pastoral Theology*. New York: Abingdon Press, 1958.)

Faith as Power

The basic source for the specific faith of pastoral counseling is the Scripture—in particular, the New Testament. For our purposes I have selected two sections of this Scripture on which to focus: one from the Epistle of James and the other from Paul's Epistle to the Romans. These provide a complementary approach in describing this faith as it effects human behavior. As a power for change, faith is described succinctly by James and dynamically by Paul. We shall focus first on James, specifically chapter 2:14-24.

This portion of Scripture was controversial during the Reformation. Martin Luther believed it undermined the Reformational doctrine of justification by grace through faith. Actually, it was already polemical when it was written. In diatribal style James engages in an argument with those in the church who he believed were distorting the meaning of faith. In the interest of faith he attacked these distortions. For James, faith is an openness to receive what God wants to give; and when it is received, it is a power for doing, for faith leads to works.

From the context it is clear what James means by works: they are activities of mercy, of compassion, of caring. The faith to which James refers is "the faith of our Lord Jesus Christ" (2:1), and the works of faith are patterned after *his* works: feeding the hungry, clothing the naked, ministering to the sick, and being an advocate for the poor and the oppressed. Faith is completed by works; that is, its purpose or meaning is fulfilled in our lives when we extend to others the compassion we receive from God through Christ. Since faith's focus is on caring, it moves us to form caring communities.

This understanding of faith is basic to the differentiation of a hearer who "forgets" and a "doer that acts" (1:25). Faith is not simply belief, not even belief in the existence of God. Nor is it belief *about* God. "Hear, O Israel, the Lord our God is one Lord" (Deut. 6:4). The Hebrews made much of their monotheism as a contrast to the henotheists and polytheists about them.

To understand the nature of faith we must go beyond its cognitive dimension—its beliefs—to its dynamic character. Faith is faith in *God*. It is an attitude of trust. Believing is different from believing a fact. Faith goes with *faith*fulness. It is not simply a realistic adaptation to reality for one's survival. Jesus' story of the rich man and Lazarus points out this difference. In this life Lazarus as a beggar ate the crumbs that fell from the rich man's table. In the next life the positions are reversed, and the rich man in misery asks Abraham to send Lazarus back to earth to warn his five brothers "lest they also come to this place." His reasoning is that if one risen from the dead goes to them they would "repent." Abraham in effect tells him it will do no good. "If they do not hear Moses and the prophets, neither will they be convinced if some one should rise from the dead" (Luke 16:19-31). They would not be convinced, in the sense of being changed persons, converted from their suspicious and arrogant ways to the way of trust and compassion; rather, they might make some patchwork adaptations to "reality," but essentially would be their same old selves. They had the opportunity in Moses and the prophets to believe —that is, to respond in faith and repent. But repentance was of no interest to them.

For James the context for faith is faith *in God*. It is relationally-centered rather than belief-centered. Beliefs are involved in faith but always as they pertain to a relationship with the *Object* of faith. The knowledge that is associated with faith (what one believes about God and how he relates to his people) has its context in *knowing* God, or as James would put it, of being "friends of God."

Resistance to Change

James assumes that through faith we have the power to act *faithfully*. If we do not, we are deceiving ourselves. Nor can we plead helplessness, for this would be an evasion of responsibility and would imply that we have a double mind. "Purify your hearts, you men of double mind" (4:8). Since Freud we describe this phenomenon as ambivalence—two strengths, wills, or minds opposing each other. The impotence that we experience from our doublemindedness is still our responsibility. "Whoever knows what is right to do and fails to do it, for him it is sin" (4:17).

There are many substitutes for action. One is *rhetoric,* a word formerly associated with a good use of words and now used pejoratively: words, words, words, but no action. Another common substitute is illness, both physical and emotional. From little on we discover that if we are sick, we are legitimately excused from certain responsibilities. It may be difficult not to exploit this "understandable excuse" when we are reluctant to act in certain distasteful or threatening circumstances.

Ironically the means for overcoming illness—"doctoring," counseling—may also become a way of evading responsibility. It should be no mystery why one can become dependent upon a physician or counselor. If one goes to a counselor, he is by that action *doing* something. From then on he may consider his problem to be the counselor's problem. Counselors who respond to this evasion of responsibility by accepting the responsibility projected onto them, simply reenforce the evasion. As the counselee quite naturally remains unchanged, the burden of the responsibility becomes increasingly heavy upon the counselor.

The most common substitute for action is waiting for the ideal conditions. Things or others have to change before *I* can change. One projects the responsibility onto others, including God, for initiating change. Until then, "I can't." Fritz Perls sounds similar to James when he says, "I can't equals I won't." The sabotage of the double mind is at work, but the resisting mind is hidden in the shades of the subconscious so that the "I can't" mind is unchallenged.

Grown people who remain dependent children often find other adults who have a parental need to take care of them. Sometimes they get married. However, "the need to take care of" can become too heavy a burden, and the "parent-mate" may begin to press the "child-mate" to "take hold."

This is what happened to a child-man we can call Martin. When his parenting wife Marilyn got tired of the burden of assuming his responsibilities, she began to resent his dependency. The more she demanded that he be responsible, the more Martin cried, "Foul!" After all, she was violating the terms of their assumed, but nonverbalized, "contract." Unfortunately he persisted in his dependency. His "I can't" was reenforced with all sorts of health problems. The marriage ended in divorce.

Power of Relationship

The power of a relationship is in the confidence and security it stimulates, whether it be a relationship within the family or with friends or with counselors. The same can be said of our relationship with God. This confidence and security is expressed in 2 Timothy 1:12: "For I know whom I have believed, and I am sure that he is able to guard until that Day what has been entrusted to me." Paul Tournier calls our relationship with God our "inner dialogue." It is no substitute for outer dialogues—relationships with people—for God is known through people who reflect his love to us. Yet the inner dialogue can be experienced in solitude; it can be a sustaining influence when external dialogues for one reason or another are not available. In this sense we are never really *alone*.

The confidence and security provided by our relationship with God is expressed most ebulliently by St. Paul: "I can do all things in him who strengthens me" (Phil. 4:13). This same Paul has also given us our most familiar expression of agonizing impotence in Romans, Chapter 7, from which we select the following representative verses:

> I do not understand my own actions. For I do not do what I want, but I do the very thing I hate (15).

> For I know that nothing good dwells within me, that is, in my flesh. I can will what is right, but I cannot do it (18).

> For I do not do the good I want, but the evil that I do not want, is what I do (19).

> Wretched man that I am! Who will deliver me from this body of death? (24)

We can easily identify with these words because they express the ruts, tapes, scripts, habit patterns that bog us down. The frustration of defeat and futility is a common human experience—often the focal pain with which pastoral counseling deals. Like Paul, some of us are too honest to deny reality, and so we suffer instead.

Because we so clearly identify with Paul's lament, one might get the impression from its frequent use that it is the culmination of the gospel. Our identification then has a negative effect, in that we inadvertently program ourselves to defeat. Yet the context of Paul's lament is hope! Defeat is not the end of his faith, but rather is the prelude to its victory. When he cries out, "Wretched man that I am! Who will deliver me from this body of death?" he already knows the answer. "Thanks be to God through Jesus Christ our Lord!" (25) As he "bottoms out" he finds his answer; the lament is over, and exaltation follows, of which Chapter 8 is an exhilarating description. "There is therefore now no condemnation for those who are in Christ Jesus. For the law of the Spirit of life in Christ Jesus has set me free from the law of sin and death" (8:1-2).

The chapter division separating Romans 7 and 8 is unfortunate because some have tended to see them separately, when in actuality the momentum from the depths of despair to the heights of joy is a dynamic continuum. The progression is plain: we experience judgment, we accept the judgment, we suffer its pain, we ask for mercy, by faith we receive it, the doors swing open, and we are exalted.

"What then shall we say to this? If God is for us, who is against us? . . . No, in all these things we are more than conquerors through him who loved us. For I am sure that neither death, nor life, nor angels, nor principalities, nor things present, nor things to come, nor powers, nor height, nor depth, nor anything else in all creation, will be able to separate us from the love of God in Christ Jesus our Lord" (Rom. 8:31-39).

Inspired with this confidence we can act, do things differently, "turn off the tapes," "change the script," direct ourselves, enter the new!

United Through Reconciliation

Paradoxically, the pursuit of the power to effect change ends in the acceptance of our powerlessness. The power for change centers in the acceptance of the self unchanged. We may not like reality, but if we are going to make a change in it, we first need to accept it. Søren Kierkegaard compares escaping from reality to movement *from the spot* and accepting reality to movement *at the spot*. Only as we move *at* the spot can we move *from* the spot. This is the direction or movement of pastoral care and counseling.

Alcoholics Anonymous incorporates this approach to reality into its First Step: "We admit we are powerless over alcohol, that our lives have become unmanageable." This is movement at the spot—the only movement that can be taken at the spot— and it applies not only to alcoholism but to whatever has us in bondage, to whatever makes us feel trapped, bound, programmed to defeat. Groups concerned with overcoming other forms of addiction, such as overeating, or with the development of a healthy emotional life, frequently use the AA steps in their programs.

In spite of the attested validity of this principle, we still try to work around it. It is hard on one's pride to admit defeat. We prefer to say that we could succeed if we really wanted to —or if we really worked at it—and these illusions may hold us together. It is not coincidental that we tend to choose these two conditions for our defense, since our cultural values support them. The work ethic that undergirds much of our culture is based upon the premise that one can accomplish almost anything one desires if one is sufficiently determined and works hard at it. High-school commencement addresses are often inspirational encouragements to believe in these principles. Change comes through willpower and hard work. There is little, if any, room in our cultural values for the ineffectiveness of work or the limitations of will power. This distortion of the purpose both of work and of the human will should not eclipse the value of either. Through our work we give expression to our creativity and contribute to the welfare of society. Through the determination and dedication of our wills we channel our resources toward our goals.

Yet the illusion of the *omnipotence* of the will overlooks the obstacle of the *divided* will. The end of doubleness does not come through willpower but through reconciliation with our divisions. The Good News which Paul extols is that God has reconciled us to himself through the life and death and resurrection of Jesus the Christ so that we might be reconciled also with ourselves and with our neighbors. Through this reconciliation a change takes place within us. As we bottom out—"o wretched man that I am, who will deliver me!" (Rom. 7:24)—the old self that was kept alive by illusions, dies. In Pauline symbols we are crucified with Christ. As he rose from the dead, we also rise with him to a new life. The will that emerges is not the old, locked into an immobilizing polarity, but a new will which is empowered by faith. Since this is a repeated experience in the dynamic for personal development, and not a once-and-for-all overcoming, the death of the old is more proleptic than final, for it is still present to harass the new. But the relationship that we have with the Spirit of God through our reconciliation is a dynamic support for continuous renewal.

Faith Utilizes the Imagination

Faith utilizes the faculty of the imagination. In fact, a functional description of faith would include this capacity for imagination. Faith stimulates the imagination to "see the picture" of hope. Jesus' parables are highly appealing to the imagination. "If you have faith as a grain of mustard seed, you will say to this mountain, 'Move hence to yonder place,' and it will move" (Matt. 17:20). Faith stimulates us to envision, and the vision challenges us to say "amen" to it. Faith focuses the imagination into a picture of anticipation. Faith programs us to victory, which is the opposite of the negative programmings of the double mind. Our actions may then follow the "track" laid in our imagination by faith. In pastoral counseling I use meditative exercises to assist the counselee in this utilization of the imagination.

The power we receive through faith to effect change applies primarily to ourselves—not to others. This may be disappointing to some counselees. They are hoping for change in husbands or wives or children or parents, and not particularly in themselves. We are prone to focus on the specks in our brother's eye rather than in the logs in our own eyes. "Why do you see the speck that is in your brother's eye, but do not notice the log that is in your own eye?" (Matt. 7:3). Yet it is precisely these logs in our own eyes that are blocking our growth. Nothing will change until we face up to their presence. "First take the log out of your own eye, and then you will see clearly to take the speck out of your brother's eye" (Matt. 7:5).

Focusing on our own logs is a painful but necessary step in our being reconciled with our total person. The power of faith to receive forgiveness for the logs in our own eyes is the power also to overcome them—to remove them. The pastoral counseling process is a dialogical dynamic that moves through reconciliation to overcoming.

God has given us the potential through his grace to change,

to grow in his likeness as revealed in Jesus Christ. This likeness is our destiny as well as our origin. We are created in God's image, and though we are fallen in sin, the *imago Dei* is still our basic identity, and we—pastor and counselee—need to affirm this identity. Through the reconciliation with our fallenness which God offers to us through Christ, we receive the power of faith to do things differently rather than to follow the same old ruts of futility. Our self-worth is a *gift* and therefore a *given*. Forgiveness grounds us in a positive realism *at the spot*. We are at the same time justified and sinners *(simul iustis et peccator)*. Such positive realism is necessary for knowing who we are.

This combination of a realistic and yet positive approach is the key to change—to growth. As Kierkegaard has pointed out, the one without the other leads ultimately to despair. In a realistic outlook alone, one sees only limits (the despair of necessity). In a positive outlook alone, one's limitless vision becomes illusion (the despair of possibility). Through forgiveness God makes available to us the gift of faith by which we can move from the spot—can overcome, change, grow—as we actualize our identity through Christ as sons and daughters of God.

Changes in ourselves also affect others, even as changes in others affect us. In this sense we do exercise an influence in the lives of others. As we have noted, the works of faith are works of compassion, of caring, of mercy. We need the support and care of others. Because of our interdependency we live in communities and worship in congregations. As a ministering body the congregation is a tremendous resource of healing power. We are usually well aware of what we have received from others during times of crisis and need. We are more likely, however, to be unaware of our continuous reception from others in non-crisis times. We are obviously influenced, *changed,* by our relationships. Yet this change is not something done for us, but rather is something in which we are involved.

A systems approach in counseling is based upon the influence of our relationships upon us. The counseling process then focuses on the interpersonal linkages involved in our conflicts and tensions. Each marriage is a system, for example, and each family. This systems pattern forms the larger context within which we can perceive, and perhaps even interpret, the substantive issues in these conflicts and tensions. Our own person is continuously being shaped by our relational systems, in which we are mutually givers and receivers. Our faith is itself a relationship-oriented power. The inner dialogue through which it functions is in turn supported, as well as influenced, by our external dialogues with caring people.

In pastoral counseling the pastor is this caring person. Yet he or she is not alone. Pastors are organically, as well as structurally, a part of a caring community. Even when pastoral counselors function in so-called "private practice," a connection between their ministry and a caring community of believers is imperative for the definition of *pastoral*. The worshiping, fellowshiping, witnessing community is a basic resource of pastoral care and counseling in its orientation to a specific faith. This community, normally localized in a congregation, provides the context for the communication, stimulation, and preservation of this faith which is a power for change. It is the therapeutic milieu that accompanies pastoral care and counseling and continues when the counseling ministry is completed. The worshiping community provides the support that the counselee needs; it is a preventative of problems and ills; it is a preservative of the faith of our Lord Jesus Christ.

Whenever one describes the local parish in such terms, one is confronted with the discrepancies to these descriptions in this or that congregation. Yet the fact that we fall short of our potentials should in no way cause us to lose sight of the congregation's basic identity as a tangible locus of the body of Christ, with its orientation in Word and sacrament, in which the members thereof minister one to another. Consequently the pastoral counseling ministry is dependent on the other ministries through which the pastor and congregation express the mission and calling of Christ.

Summary

The uniqueness of pastoral counseling in its relationship to pastoral care centers in the specific faith that distinguishes pastoral care and counseling from the rationale of other helping disciplines. As a power for change, this faith is based on the Good News of God's unconditional love revealed in the life, death, and resurrection of Christ. The reconciliation effected by God through Christ can liberate one from the bondage of defeat so that one may affirm one's identity as a son or daughter of God. This faith rests on the covenant that God initiates with us by his grace, a covenant comparable to marriage and established by the sacrament of Baptism. This covenant is dynamically a relationship between the Spirit of God and the human spirit. It constitutes an inner dialogue that can sustain one's hope in the midst of crises which would otherwise point only to the emptiness and meaninglessness of life. The purpose of pastoral care and counseling is to catalyze and to support this covenanted capacity for dialogue with its focus on hope.

The specific faith of pastoral care and counseling is organically related to a worshiping and witnessing community within which pastoral care and counseling are ministries. It is the cognitive deposit that shapes these pastoral ministries and which in turn is shaped also by them. We turn now to a development of the *reconciliation* dimension of this theology in its application to pastoral care and counseling.

3

Guilt
and
Reconciliation

Pulitzer Prize writer John Cheever said, "Regret, sadness, are very much a part of my life. But so is the endless pursuit of summer, which one carries on with a good deal of vitality." In contrast, a public figure of the entertainment world who has experienced several divorces and had severe bouts with chemical dependency, said, "I have never had any regrets." The difference between these two people is in their response to guilt, which in turn determines whether one can profit from experience—whether one can change.

Guilt as a Human Phenomenon

One reason why the specific faith of pastoral care and counseling is called Gospel or Good News is because it affirms reconciliation to the guilty through the forgiveness of sin. The prevalence of alienation and loneliness, together with the debilitating effects of a low self-image, are all related directly or indirectly to unresolved guilt. Guilt can be defined both subjectively and objectively. In the Bible guilt usually refers to one's status before God. Hence it is an objective guilt. A typical example is the statement of James, "Whoever keeps the whole law but fails in one point has become guilty of all of it"

(James 2:10). We have this same objective understanding of guilt as a transgression of law in our human juridical system.

Though pronounced guilty by the court of law, however, the convicted person may insist, "I am innocent." Conversely, one who believes himself to be guilty may be assured by others, even by the court, that he or she is *not* guilty. In the ministry of the church there is this same subjective–objective tension in regard to guilt before God. One's interpretation of his or her offense may seem to others more like an excuse than a confession, while another's interpretation may seem excessively severe. Regardless of these differences in interpretation, however, we can define guilt subjectively as an uncomfortable awareness of a contrast between one's behavior and/or one's being and what one's behavior and/or one's being should be in one's self-assessment.

Even at the subjective level, guilt needs to be distinguished from guilt *feelings*. As a negative judgment upon oneself due to one's awareness of a transgression, guilt has rational content. Guilt feelings, on the other hand, are generated in response to this judgment.

Guilt may have a corporate as well as an individual focus. Members of a particular group, for example, may share a common negative judgment about themselves. The group member may accept this judgment as his or her own in addition to whatever guilt one has over one's own responsibilities as an individual. Guilt may be subconscious as well as conscious. Ironically, when it is subconscious, it may affect our behavior as much as, or even more than, when it is conscious.

Religiously speaking, guilt is a breach in our relationships— particularly with God. It is precipitated as we are convicted by our own awareness that we have violated or evaded our obligations to others and ultimately to God—that we "have sinned and fall short of the glory of God" (Rom. 3:23). Although psychologically, guilt is my own judgment on my own unacceptableness, it is also frequently my awareness of a transcendent dimension to this judgment. While some may not identify this transcendent awareness with the judgment of God, they may still sense an obligation to more than themselves or to other people. The Alcoholics Anonymous concept of the *higher Power* is probably the best clinical term for this awareness. For many people the symbol God is loaded with unresolved guilt and resentment from their past experiences, and this is often true of the chemically dependent. Though *higher Power* is used synonymously with *God* in the Twelve Steps of AA, some chemically dependent persons will respond positively to *higher Power* but negatively to *God*.

That we human beings are aware of guilt is an indication of our freedom and our responsibility to this freedom. In its religious context guilt is a consequence of our having sinned. Sins are defined as those of commission (what I have done but should not have done) and those of omission (what I have not done but should have done). There is both a helpless and responsible side to sin. Like the alcoholic, those burdened by other negative compulsions may refer to their impotency as "the bondage of sin." At the same time, the Christian understanding of sin is based on the reality of human freedom. As defined by Søren Kierkegaard, sin is a *position* and not a *negation*: that is, it is a decisive act and not a capitulation through weakness. Our guilt, then, is our own negative evaluation of our actions or inactions—that we not only should, but could, have done differently.

In the clinical field William Glasser's Reality Therapy reflects this same responsibility for behavior and criticizes psychiatric approaches that attribute negative behavior to sickness. When a client informs Glasser that he or she feels guilty, he is inclined to inform them that they probably have good reason for feeling this way (*Reality Therapy*. New York: Harper and Row, 1965, p. 79).

Kurt Adler, son of Alfred Adler, who follows his father's approach, sees the same purpose for the sickness label as does

Glasser, but he views its purpose differently. We label behavior as sick, he says, to reduce our guilt feelings. Alcoholism is called a disease, though there is no psysiological evidence for this. Yet if one is sick, he or she cannot be responsible and therefore cannot be guilty. Why do we need to reduce guilt in alcoholism? Because guilt is a barrier to breaking with the addiction. In fact, Adler sees guilt feelings as a substitute for change. He illustrates the point with the following story. After listening to the lament of a young man that he was masturbating and was feeling guilty about it, Adler said, "You are masturbating *and* feeling guilty! That's not fair! Do one or the other, but not both."

Both Glasser and Adler are critical of the Freudian view of guilt as an inevitable tension between one's biological and social selves. In his *Civilization and Its Discontents,* Freud views society as the enemy of individuality, which he associates with spontaneity. The *id,* representing the biological self, and the *superego,* representing the psychological internalization of societal mores, are terms descriptive of the adversaries in the conflict, and the *ego* is the potential arbiter between them. Society then exploits the *superego*'s judgment upon the *id* to control the individual. The ontological nature of this conflict is also reflected by the philosopher Schopenhauer who compared persons to porcupines who huddle together for warmth but draw back again because of the pricks of the quills.

Erik Erikson makes a distinction between guilt and shame, with shame coming to the fore during the anal period of development, when the child exercises its autonomy and experiences rejection by the significant others in its life. Humiliated by this exposure, the child wishes to be swallowed up. Guilt, on the other hand, develops in the later phallic period, when one's initiative unfolds and brings one into conflict with these same significant others. Thus, guilt refers more to one's *doing,* while shame applies primarily to one's *being.* As an indictment of one's total being, shame is comparable to the contemporary clinical term, low self-image. Though it centers in the realm of being, the low self-image extends its effect into the realm of doing. Shame is expressed by Paul in the culmination of his lament over his guilt. "Wretched man that I am! Who will deliver me from this body of death?" (Rom. 7:24).

The psychic mechanism for guilt, called the superego by Freud, is more traditionally labeled the *conscience*. "Let your conscience be your guide" implies that conscience embodies our moral and ethical standards for behavior. Going against these standards gives one a "guilty conscience." While any claim to universal or inherent behavioral standards would be contested, it is generally agreed that the potential for internalizing such standards is universal. Though these standards are received from parent-type authorities during the developing years, the dynamics for this value-oriented internalization is inherent in human nature and perhaps also in some animal life.

Sociopathic persons are often described as lacking a conscience since they seem to be incapable of guilt or remorse in their behavioral transgressions of community standards. In Berne's terms, they have not developed a "parent ego state." There is some evidence, however, that rather than lacking a conscience, the sociopathic person has repressed it. (Cf. Wayne Oates, *Anxiety in Christian Experience* and Edmund Stein, *Guilt, Its Theory and Therapy*.) For example, sociopathic persons are frequently intolerant of their own company and therefore of any reflective activity which would bring them into close contact with themselves.

Since guilt as an experience begins very early in one's existence, its presence can easily become a habit pattern. The question is whether our guilt is a response to our awareness of personal failure or whether we project the image of failure onto the way we perceive ourselves. One reason that guilt may become a habit is that parents and other authorities often attempt to stimulate it as a way of punishing or controlling a child. As the child internalizes these authorities into its parent ego state, the child has developed the dynamics for the continuous presence of guilt. While guilt is uncomfortable, its absence may be not only strange but frightening. That to which we become habituated becomes part of our security system—what Karen Horney calls "the security of the familiar."

In spite of its morbid gratification, guilt is a state of mind in which we are "down" on ourselves. As a counselee put it, "A number of people I know have a low self-image, being nervous, insecure, threatened and defensive. They really know who they are, and being repulsed, cannot be reconciled to themselves. I see the same struggle haunting myself, and it overshadows my relationship to God and to others. Being insecure, many of my relationships are 'clingy.' " A recent study of women in prison, whose objective guilt was evidenced by their incarceration, revealed that they had virtually no sense of self-worth. In their insecurity they had become dependent persons—often on men, who in turn exploited their vulnerability. In a similar way marital partners whose low self-esteem moves them to a demanding dependency on their spouses, are sowing the seeds through this dependency for the dissolution of their marriage.

When our guilt is manifested in low self-esteem, we have an underlying conviction of worthlessness. An even heavier indictment is that of phoniness. The older word is *hypocrisy* which means literally, *hidden under*. Because we can use our communicative abilities to deceive as well as to reveal, we can hide behind our exterior, covering our negative identity. Despite our success with others in this deception, we may be trapped, nevertheless, by our own awareness of incongruity, and the indictment leaves its imprint on our psyche.

If we are to be liberated from the bondage of guilt, the conflict over ourselves implicit in guilt needs to be resolved. If guilt has a religious dimension—and I believe it has—this resolution needs to take seriously this element of transcendence. We cannot eliminate guilt as though we were our own god; rather it is "eternity's demand on us" (Kierkegaard). Karen Horney describes the bondage of guilt as the "tyranny of the should." Simply to defy our guilt by our behavior may only alienate us further from our own identity.

The Punitive Approach

Because guilt implies judgment, we have attempted to resolve it by punitive means, as punitive parents behave toward their guilty child. The guilty must be punished to pay the penalty for their sins. In administering this punishment to ourselves we are following a course befitting our low self-image, and using the juridical system model as the way in which we relate to ourselves. This course is self-destructive, as we sabotage our own goals to "placate the gods."

The punitive approach may be a direct infliction of pain or of what otherwise is negative, or a denial of privilege—withholding the positive. Guilt *feelings,* which in themselves are miserable, may serve this purpose. In his autobiography, the Russian religious philosopher Nicolai Berdyaev confessed, "Every joy in my life has been accompanied by a sense of guilt and wrong." His image of himself did not permit an unalloyed joy.

Yet one is seeking something other than punishment in self-punishment; one is seeking security. Actually the self-punisher fears a greater punishment. After King David took a census of his people, "his heart smote him," because he had done it out of pride. The prophet Gad offered him his choice of punishment by God or by his enemies. David answered, "I am in great distress, let us fall into the hand of the Lord, for his mercy is great; but let me not fall into the hand of man" (2 Sam. 24:14). Self-punishers resist any such choice; they want to do the job themselves. Even masochists who seek punishment from others are seeking punishment they can control.

Security comes from being in control of the punishment one deserves.

The punitive approach to guilt distorts the purpose of guilt. As a tension over the contrast between the way we are and the way we believe we should be, guilt is a stimulus for change. When we resort to self-punishment to ease the tension, we are in effect paying a debt. Self-punishment is a substitute for change—for growth.

Gail Sheehy in *Passages* says that for our personal maturation we need to leave the "inner custodian," the punishing parent. But how does one do this? How does one break the chains which one has helped to forge? The portrayal of a psychiatrist in a prominent motion picture, as she was confronted by the admission of a grieving divorcee that she felt guilty, illustrates the problem. The psychiatrist's answer was, "Don't feel guilty." This makes as much psychiatric sense as saying to the anxiety ridden, "Don't worry," or to those obsessed by rage, "Don't be angry," or to those sunk in despair, "Don't be depressed."

How is one to overcome guilt when one is acually overcome by it? Appeals to willpower are ludicrous when the will itself is in bondage. Paula and Dick McDonald in *Guilt-Free* suggest that since we have internalized our standards from authority figures in our lives, we may need an authority figure to free us from their judgment. "Seek a permission giving minister," they advise. The implication is that since religion brought it in, it takes religion to get rid of it. The clergy's symbolic role distinguishes them from other helping professionals in this emancipation from the bondage of guilt.

Denial of Guilt

Some persons have a difficult time admitting to guilt. Their defensiveness is in effect saying, "I'm innocent. You can't blame me!" Perhaps there have been too many old and painful memories associated with it. They may not even like to use the word *guilt.* They either narrow its definition so that it does not apply to them, or they call it by some less offensive synonym.

This resistance to guilt can move one to deny it when it is present. The guilt, then, becomes manifested in other tensions, which though distressing, are less threatening.

One of these is anger. Some respond to guilt with anger, as though guilt put them on the defensive and they then take to the offensive.

Another tension behind which guilt may be concealed is anxiety, often referred to simply as *tension.* Since guilt includes the fear of judgment, anxiety is a logical displacement.

A third cover-up is depression. Paul Pruyser says that depression is a clinical term, and the term associated with the pastoral tradition is sadness. It is Pruyser's contention that pastors should diagnose as well as counsel in the light of their own heritage of theology rather than with the borrowed perceptions of psychotherapy. While I agree with this position, I also believe that the word *depression,* despite its origins, is now commonplace in our vocabulary. Depression is often described as anger turned inward. While this is too simple a definition, it has an element of truth. The guilty self is a logical target for anger because self-accusation is already present. In fact, depression—like low self-esteem—may be a specific manifestation of guilt.

When guilt is hidden behind these other tensions, it is a further step removed from resolution. If the displacement is anger, one's energies are directed in an attack on external targets. If it is *tension,* or anxiety, we are drawn to our culturally conditioned remedy: take a sedative or tranquilizer—"pop a pill." Though depression may be closer to guilt than these other displacements, the debilitating effects of depression undermine one's ability to cope. Again, the cultural remedy is drugs. Though drugs may be helpful, at least temporarily, they do not resolve the guilt, and they can be addictive.

We can deny our guilt also by projecting it into our relationships. Our lack of acceptance is projected onto others who manifest our unacceptable characteristics. When we attack others, we could with good reason say, "There go I!" Since our guilt is an obstacle to becoming intimate with ourselves, its projection into our relationships is an obstacle to intimacy with others. The way we relate to ourselves serves as a model for the way we relate to others. We tend to love our neighbor as we love ourselves.

Guilt may be denied also by transferring one's conscience to the consensus of groups or institutions. That to which we would not consent as individuals, we may accept if it is endorsed by a group or institution to which we adhere. The scandals associated with governmental agencies in which people steal millions of dollars through "kick backs" and "overcharges," is one example. "Official corruption" of this magnitude is possible only because the consciences of individuals who otherwise are law-abiding persons are rationalized by the institutional consensus that stealing from the government is not really stealing—not really a crime, not really a sin—particularly when it is the accepted practice. In fact, one may be made to feel stupid if one does not participate in the "opportunity."

The way in which religious cults "take over" the consciences of their members is another example. Individuals who would be repulsed even by the *thought* of murder may so idolize their leader that they would "kill for him or her." Though the leader's behavior may deviate from standards held by the individual members of the group, the individual as a member of the group has a need to protect the leader, even if only by granting him or her the divine right to be different. Both leader and followers, therefore, give social and religious support to the rationalization of evil and the denial of guilt.

The Christian Approach—Forgiveness

The Christian approach to the bondage of sin and guilt is appropriately called the Good News. The news is that God has acted and is acting to deliver us from our bondage. The Christian approach, consequently, takes seriously the transcendent dimension of guilt: it is guilt before God. It also takes seriously human fallenness—the radical evil at the heart of humanity. The bondage to guilt is due to a prior bondage to sin, and only God can break this bondage. The Good News is that God through Christ has forgiven our sins.

The public response to Transactional Analysis in its proclamation of "I'm OK; You're OK," shows how great is the desire to feel good about ourselves. Conversely, it shows how "down" we are on ourselves and others. While there are parallels between being OK and being forgiven, they are not the same. The gospel offers forgiveness to those who are sinners— who are not OK. George Forell is credited with depicting Jesus on the cross saying to the jeering crowd beneath him, "If I'm OK and You're OK, what am I doing hanging here!" The radical evil in human nature put Christ on the cross, and yet through that cross God offers to us his reconciliation. In the initiatory rite of Baptism, water is used to symbolize our need for cleansing. In the sacrament of Holy Communion, bread and wine are used as symbols of Christ's broken body and shed blood, to indicate our need for redemption. As a corporate sacrament the Holy Communion is a dramatic demonstration that the way is also cleared for reconciliation in our human relationships.

The way of forgiveness does not gloss over painful realities; rather forgiveness is received through repentance, the first step of which is confession. The New Testament word for repentance—*metanoia*—means a change of mind. Repentance is our response to our guilt and marks a break with our past. For-

giveness draws the curtain on the past, giving one permission
to leave old ways and to enter into new ones.

For those of us whose guilt is manifested as a low self-image,
the gospel is God's revelation of our personal worth. God's love
is demonstrated in his self-giving—"He so loved that he gave"
—and by this action he declared not only his love but also our
worth. "Nothing greater can happen to a human being," says
Paul Tillich in *The New Being,* "than that he is forgiven."
Why? Because "forgiveness means reconciliation in spite of
estrangement; it means reunion in spite of hostility; it means
acceptance of those who are unacceptable, and it means reception of those who are rejected. In the ecstasy of this experience,
St. Paul exults, "If God is for us, who is against us?" (Rom.
8:31). If God can forgive us, we can—we are called upon—to
forgive ourselves.

The Good News that God is for us can be a stabilizing influence in our personal relationships. Bill, for example, was losing
what little confidence he had through the deterioration of his
marriage. His wife had a lover and was undecided about continuing the marriage. Bill tried desperately to please her: he
was docile, accommodating. When this approach failed to
bring any change in the situation, Bill became angry and
accusatory. His pastor suggested that before Bill could work
on his marriage he needed to work on himself. He helped him
to see that his dependency on his wife, in addition to hindering
his marriage was an indication of his own low image of himself. He was depending on his marriage for his identity. In his
"undemanding" way Bill was actually demanding too much
and consequently giving too little.

With Bill's consent the pastor focused on Bill's relationship
to God, and assisted him in developing a devotional discipline
that would help him to receive the assurance of worth. As his
awareness of his own identity increased, Bill became less anxious about his marriage. "I still want her very much," he said,
"but I could survive if it did not work out." As might be antici-

pated, his personal growth in confidence made him more attractive to his wife.

Reliving to Reconciliation

Because of the painful memories that may accompany confession and the denial processes that we use to protect us from this pain, some may need the personal ministry of pastoral counseling to assist in the realization of God's forgiveness. In the presence of another, one may need to *relive* the painful memories. Reliving is a form of confession, and like confession, can lead to reconciliation. For several years I asked the same member of Alcoholics Anonymous to speak to my class in pastoral care. I apologized for asking so frequently for the same service. "Don't apologize," he said. "I get something out of it too. Each time I tell my story I die a little more to it."

Those grieving over the death of a loved one may be burdened by guilt as well. This is particularly true when the death was sudden. The bereaved may think of many things in their relationship with the deceased which they wish they could "live over." "If only I had—if only I had not—." The counseling pastor may need to listen to these "if onlys" over and again, until the person is finally able to "let them go."

Reliving is more than relating or narrating. Some people become chronic confessors who tell their story to one pastor after another. There is no emancipation from their guilt because their "confession" is for manipulatory purposes. To relive is to tell one's story within the context, including the "feeling tone," of the trauma that accompanied it. Since the reliving takes place in the milieu of a positive relationship—often in contrast to the original setting—it can dispose one toward reconciliation.

Sometimes the conflict is too threatening to relive. The emotions and images associated with it are repressed, so that the individual has difficulty in recalling. The counselor may utilize the technique of role-play in these instances, to relieve the blockage. Besides being a helpful method in the teaching of counseling, role-play is also a good counseling method. If, for example, the pastor can pick up enough of the context to re-enact the role of an offending person in a traumatic situation, the pastor can suggest to the counselee that they role-play the relationship. The counselee plays him or herself with the intent of becoming aware of the feelings involved. Although coun-selees may discover through the role-play that they are unable to express these feelings because of their intensity, they are obviously aware of them, and reveals them nonverbally to the sensitive counselor, who then can respond to them and reflect on them after the role-play.

Role-play can also be used to penetrate other forms of denial. A student counselor, for example, decided to use role-play to end an impasse in his counseling with a married couple. For several sessions he had listened to the wife charge her husband with infidelity and to the husband vehemently deny it. As a way also of relieving his own frustration, the student suggest-ed that the husband take the role of the wife while she stood behind him, and he would take the husband's role. The hus-band (as his wife) began by accusing the counselor (the hus-band) of infidelity, and the counselor defended himself. Within a few minutes they were vehemently involved in the dialogue. In fact, the husband became so involved that he destroyed the counselor's (his own) defenses. When he realized what had happened, he sighed and said, "Let's stop. There's no use to go on. I may as well talk about it. I've been seeing a woman. It's been going on for two years, and I don't know what to do."

Not all guilt should be taken at face value. While guilt is real, as Hobart Mowrer insists, it may also be neurotic. The in-tensity of the guilt may be out of proportion to what is sup-posedly causing it. People who feel intensely guilty over minor, or even imagined, violations of religious, social, or ethical obli-gations may be suffering from neurotic guilt. The guilt is genuine, but the issue to which it is fixed is usually a substitute. The minor violation is a surface or safe concern on which to deposit a heavy burden of guilt. The person holds on to the substitute because it is a protection from facing a more painful judgment. The real source of the guilt may be a repressed anger or hatred toward loved ones or even toward God, or some similarly threatening transgression. Hostility is difficult for us to cope with in our culture. More easily forgivable sins, consequently, are tempting "hooks" upon which to hang the guilt.

A woman in her sixties had visited most of the clergy in her community seeking help for having committed "the sin against the Holy Ghost." The clergy would assure her that since she was worried about it, she obviously had not committed it. This relieved her—for about fifteen minutes. Subsequently she was admitted to a mental hospital where she received many shock treatments. Finally she was moved to the custodial ward of the hospital as a more or less permanent patient. When an advanced student of mine asked for a tough assignment I suggested this woman.

She began as usual to confess the sin against the Holy Ghost, but he did not try as others to reassure her. Instead he asked her why she thought she was guilty of it. "Thoughts," she said.

"What thoughts?" he asked. She opened the door of her room to see if anyone was listening. "Afraid someone will hear?" She nodded.

When spring came, he took her outside and pointed to the large grounds where no one could possibly eavesdrop, asked, "Can you tell me your thoughts now?" She shook her head no.

"Could you write them?" He offered her a pencil. She made no comment but hesitatingly opened her purse and began writing on a paper handkerchief. Looking over her shoulder he saw that she had written, "Goddamn you! Get the hell out of here!"

Realizing that he had seen it, she crumbled the paper, put it in her mouth and swallowed it. "I saw it," he said with a smile. "You surely are angry with me, aren't you?"

This breakthrough marked the beginning of a new relationship in which the counselor heard less and less about the sin against the Holy Ghost and more and more about her anger over her lot in life. Because he was able to accept her hostility toward him, he helped her to transfer her conflict with God and with people to the counseling relationship, where the encounter could be therapeutic. The reconciliation she experienced with the counselor became a model for reconciliation with God and with herself. Also for a person so repressed, the direct expression of her hostility was in itself an integrating experience—especially since it was accepted. Her mental condition improved, and she was released from the hospital. For years afterward she maintained a relatively interdependent existence as a "cleaning lady" in the community.

Besides being neurotic, guilt may also be dated. The conscience standards upon which it is based may no longer be considered appropriate by the individual, and yet the consciousness of guilt continues due to the emotional fixation to an earlier conditioning. Such a person needs someone to give him or her permission to disregard the conscience at this point. This is a task for which the authority implicit in the symbolic role of the pastor is uniquely fitted. When visiting with a former counselee, I was reminded by him of the time when I told him to tell his conscience to "go to hell for Christ's sake." Frankly I could not recall saying this. Since he had been a perfectionist who drove himself unmercifully and then berated himself for falling short, I could imagine myself saying it. It was a type of exorcism. *He* recalled it because it aided him in distinguishing the proddings of his dated conscience from the Word of God.

There are several ways by which theologians describe how and why the cross is a symbol of our reconciliation. What unites all of these metaphors is the Good News that atonement has been made. There is no need, therefore, for the guilty to make their own. There is no need for self-inflicted sufferings, for programming oneself to failure, for suicidal sabotage, nor even for a family scapegoat. The pastor can provide people with these destructive tendencies with the permission they need to put the "whip" on the shelf. When I so encouraged one such counselee, he said, "I'm going to do more than that. I'm going to break it in pieces and burn it!"

A Needed Tension

Theologically speaking, the tyrannizing conscience is conscience under the law, while the freedom we have through Christ places the conscience under the gospel. In relational analogues, the tyrannizing conscience is the internalized punitive parent harassing either a rebellious or a conforming child. Emancipation through the gospel does not eliminate this parent-child tension, but rather changes it from a destructive to a constructive tension. We still have a parent within us—and a child, but the relationship between them is liberated from the distorting power struggle of two opposing ego-states to a constructive dialogue. We are still under obligations—responsibilities—in terms of our identity as children of God.

The dialogue is illustrated by the child trait of honesty, for example, with the parental trait of commitment. Both are basic to human identity, and each needs the other for protection from distortion. Jesus' ordeal in the Garden of Gethsemane is an example of honesty and commitment in constructive tension. Although he had "set his face to go to Jerusalem," Jesus was in anguish over this decision on the eve of his death. He felt like backing out. "Father, if thou art willing, remove this cup from me." He faced his desire to avoid the cross honestly with himself and God. With the ambivalence out in the open he made the decision to carry through with his commitment. "Nevertheless, not my will, but thine, be done" (Luke 22:40-42). From the pain of this ordeal he was strengthened to go to the cross. It is in part the pain that comes from "listening to our own voices." By being honest about his feelings and desires and yet clear about his commitment, he was victorious over his temptation as the *last Adam* (1 Cor. 15:45).

Commitment is deemphasized in our day. We have liberated the "child" but muzzled the "parent" in the process—literally as well as symbolically. In a recent study concerning the problems of discipline in our schools, the conclusion reached was that "the teacher is the major cause of classroom difficulties." A similar conclusion seems to be reached regarding conflicts between the parent and child within us. Freed from the parent's domination, the child is committed primarily to its own fulfillment, but it lacks the parental qualities. The child trait of honesty is elevated to top status among the virtues. It justifies all sorts of misconduct, the gratification of our desires, and even arrogance and cruelty. "At least I'm honest," is an accepted defense for many behavioral aberrations. It is the current version of the Pharisee's prayer "with himself" (Luke 18:9-14). "I thank thee, Lord, that I am not like others who are dishonest and hypocritical. I say what I think—regardless of whom it hurts." The husband in the previous chapter, who was determined to follow his desires "no matter who gets hurt," is an example of this emancipation. Since the quality of honesty by itself lacks direction, it can easily foster our egocentricity.

"Doing my own thing," seeking my own fulfillment no matter who gets hurt, undermines the spirit of cooperation and community. Our present binge in this direction is really a caricatured revival of American rugged individualism. Interdependence is scorned, not simply as a mark of weakness, but as an infringement on personal rights. Without social obligations there are fewer checks on our egocentricity. This defiance of responsibility to others ultimately backs us into the corner of loneliness and alienation.

Our deemphasis on commitment is a reaction to a previous day of child repression and parental dominance. The child in

us was too low in self-esteem to claim its own space. The reaction to this deflation of the child is an inflated child that
owns no responsibility to the family or the community. These
are opposite sides of the same coin, the result of a breakdown
in dialogue between parent and child. We have a commitment
to others—a responsibility to family and community, as well as
to our own personal fulfillment. This needed dialectic between honesty and commitment, parent and child, law and
freedom, may mean at times self-denial rather than self-grati-
fication, sacrifice rather than fulfilling desires.

To become responsible persons we need to listen to all of our
inner voices in order to discover our true identity. Like many
others, a young woman, whom we can call Betty, asked for
counseling because she was unhappy over events in her life and
not because she felt guilty. She had developed a very possessive
relationship with a girl friend with whom she shared an apart-
ment. Her jealous demands finally destroyed the relationship.
Now, rejected and alone, she sought help. As her rapport with
the counselor developed, she hinted at a deeper concern. Although there had been no overt sexual overtures, she was questioning whether she was homosexual. She admitted to much
guilt over this possibility, but was not sure whether this guilt
was culturally conditioned or whether it was because she was
acting contrary to her own identity. One thing was certain: it
was guilt at its destructive dimension, for it simply fixed her
where she was.

Actually, Betty's attachment to her friend proved to be more
an indication of her personal immaturity than of homosexu-
ality. Childlike in her possessiveness, she was resisting growing up. Her childhood had been unfulfilled. She was one of
the younger children in a large family whose security was
constantly undermined by parental friction. In the midst of
successive family crises Betty received very little attention from
anyone. We can best leave any stage of life after we have ex-

perienced fulfillment in it. When this is not the case, we persist
—often pathologically—to obtain what was missed.

After they had had several sessions together, the counselor
decided to bring Betty's conflict to a head. He put the question to her, "If you could have what you wanted, what would
you choose?" He, the authority, the pastor, the adult, was offering her freedom. At first she reacted like any child who gets
an unexpected privilege. Looking at him skeptically, she said,
"You mean if I really could have what I want?"

"Yes."

"Well, then, I would want my girlfriend back."

The counselor accepted her decision. "If this is what you
want, the matter is settled. It's a question then of putting your
efforts in this direction."

Betty was confused. The pastor was not offering any resistance. This was not the authority role she had anticipated.
There was no game to play, no parent to outwit, no "mother-
ing giant" to protect her. She had to become the parent of
her own child.

"Maybe it's not just that," she said. "I mean, well, I'd like to
get married too—and have children."

When she realized she had the opportunity to remain a
child, it was no longer attractive. The adult came forth.

At the concluding session Betty expressed appreciation for
the help she had received. "The turning point," she said, "was
that question you asked me—you know—if I could really have
what I wanted, what would I want? Well, I'd never thought of
it that way before." What she meant by "that way" was "outside the framework of the game" that had fixed her to a child
level of relating to authority. Now that the authority had re-
fused to play the game, she saw that with freedom came responsibility. There were consequences for which there was no protection. She had to become a responsible person to achieve her
goals.

Liberated for Change

Liberation from the bondage of sin and guilt means being able to do what one could not do before. When we leave the old to enter the new, this means new *doing*. In harmony with the implicit purpose of guilt, reconciliation makes possible change in behavior. As a change of mind, repentance is the initial step in this change of direction. We *live out* our forgiveness on the human scene. Its most immediate effect is to move us to extend this same forgiveness to others. The Lord's Prayer is our most familiar description of this reciprocity: "Forgive us our trespasses as we forgive those who trespass against us." The Sermon on the Mount contains a similar expression: "So if you are offering your gift at the altar, and there remember that your brother has something against you, leave your gift there before the altar and go; first be reconciled to your brother, and then come and offer your gift" (Matt. 5:23-24).

In a television interview with Mike Wallace on *Sixty Minutes,* Charles Colson, following his conversion to Christianity, was asked if he had apologized to the people he had attacked in his role as a reputed "hatchet man" in the Nixon administration. Colson dodged the question by replying that Christ had forgiven him. Wallace countered, "A new Christian, besides talking to his God, does he do no penance for deeds like that?" Colson admitted that Wallace had scored hard. He had made his new faith a "cop-out" from his personal responsibilities to other people. Wallace, in effect, was saying, "First be reconciled to your brother."

Reconciliation with God frees us from bondage to our past so that we may do things differently in the present. The legendary Casey Stengel said of one of his ballplayers, "When he gets mad, he thinks only of the last play instead of the next one." This is what unresolved guilt does to us: it fixes our attention on the negatives of the past so that we repeat our failures rather than overcome them. Freud observed this tendency and called it the *repetition compulsion*. It is a tragic waste of human potential, reflecting inability to profit from experience.

If God has removed our transgressions "as far as the east is from the west" (Ps. 103:12), he also removed their power to perpetuate themselves. With the bondage to sin and guilt removed, we are free to move in a different direction. Forgiveness makes possible the "healing of the memories" so that their influence no longer predestines our behavior. A pastoral counselor may be needed to assist in this emancipation. By reaffirming the Good News through his or her supportive relationship, the pastor can help the counselee to release the "snags" that continue by the familiarity of habit to bind one to old ways. He or she can reenforce the counselee's desire to abandon dated resistances and to risk new action. In a dialogue about self-image the counselee may see more of the "hardened crud" that clings negatively to it despite God's declaration of justification and reconciliation.

When we are liberated through the Good News from the bondage of guilt, we can use our guilt to enhance our understanding of ourselves. Relieved of its judgment, guilt provides us with our own feedback on our behavior. By reliving the healed memory, we may gain insight into the old tapes, defensive reactions, fears, and irritations that sabotage our self-direction. We need this understanding to change our ways. The pastor may encourage the counselee to keep a journal of these insights so that they become fixed in his or her mind. In addition to reliving the old, we can use our imagination to live it differently. We can envision ourselves functioning as we wish we had. We redo it with *new* doing. One way of doing this is through the medium of meditation which will be discussed in a later chapter. This trial run in the mind helps us to break up old patterns in our thinking. We are more likely, then, to act in this new way in a real situation. When such "victories" occur, they too need to be recorded in the journal.

We can learn by reflecting on our victories as well as on our failures.

When guilt has served its purpose, we need to let it go. Ironically, we may instead hold on to it. It may seem strange to be without it. As uncomfortable as it is, our consciousness of guilt may be providing us with "the security of the familiar." We need to hear the call of God to surrender it—to leave the old with its security of habit and to risk entering into new possibilities. Pastoral counseling may provide the needed support for people to release their hold on old and destructive ways. It takes courage to go where we have not yet been, and most of us need reassurance from those who have been there.

Receivers Need Also to Give

Those who have received need also to give. Helping institutions, from the government to the church, tend to forget this. Tillich says that "people are sick not only because they have not received love, but also because they are not allowed to give it." Our self-image is elevated not only through receiving, but also through giving. Only with God can we be primarily receivers —without damaging our self-image. Our human relationships prosper only where there is a mutuality of giving and receiving.

While we vary in the kind of gifts we can offer, all gifts are enhanced when the giver gives also him or her self. The gospel focuses our worth on our person and not on our achievements. God has justified our person, our being, by his grace. Yet we tend to experience our most intense inferiority over our person. This is why we feel more comfortable when we know what to *do* or to *say* in any particular situation. We have a need to do or say something to justify our existence. But before we *do,* we need to *be.* We need to believe in the worth of our person, our presence. This is our basic offering also in our pastoral counseling.

The gift of *presence* is often withheld when it is most needed. The lonely, the sick, the elderly, the disturbed, all need the presence of people. Our daughter died in a hospital because, in her great need for the presence of another person, she was given instead a drug. The elderly are particularly forsaken because they have been displaced from the mainstream of life. They need the presence of others if they are to continue to believe in their own worth. Instead they too are often given drugs instead.

The therapy of Alcoholics Anonymous includes this mutuality of giving and receiving. Those who receive help from others are obligated to respond to those who need it. Eric Berne believes this reciprocity is simply a switch in roles of the same game. The victim is now the rescuer and is just as dependent on another victim as he or she was before on the rescuer. While one can distort most transactions into a game, reciprocity itself is no game. One is offering what one is particularly qualified to give. Who can better understand an alcoholic than one who is a sober alcoholic? Who then is in a better position to help? The same can be said for other forms of human suffering. Those uniquely qualified to minister to the grieving, for example, are those who have endured a similar loss. The help they received in their pain is the help they now wish to give. "Freely ye have received, freely give" (Matt. 10:8 KJV). With these words Jesus sent out his disciples to minister to those in need. The security we have in our being through receiving leads to creativity in our giving—our doing.

The pastoral counselor is also a pastoral administrator. It is his or her challenge to provide concrete ways in which people can contribute of themselves. The counselee is potentially a giver. Through their awareness of people who have suffered and have overcome, pastors have a potential "bank" of sensitive and caring persons which they can utilize as an extension of the ministry of the church. Those who have received through pastoral counseling will continue to receive as they give counsel to others. Again, this is especially true in respect to the elderly. As victims of our patronizing care, they rarely have the opportunity to contribute to others. The pastor is in a unique position to assist these veterans-in-living to contribute what they have experienced to those in need of this understanding in critical moments. We will discuss further this administrative challenge in the final chapter.

Summary

The specific faith that undergirds pastoral care and counseling has a major focus in God's initiation of reconciliation with his people through the forgiveness of sin. This Good News is a liberating power for those of us in bondage to the variety of self-sabotaging ways by which we attempt to keep our guilt appeased. It is this message of reconciliation—of God's unconditional love—that is communicated and reenforced, verbally and nonverbally, in pastoral care and counseling. The result of its reception is an ever renewable potential for the freedom to be and to become. Reconciliation is received through the medium of confession and repentance. Confession in the form of reliving is inherent in the pastoral counseling process, enhanced by such techniques as role-playing and role-reversal. The change of mind that constitutes repentance can lead also to a change in behavior. Through forgiveness one can do things *differently*. Reconciliation releases the power for new doing. The pastor may assist this new doing by providing tangible ways for those who have received love to give it.

4

Death
and
Resurrection

The specific faith of pastoral care and counseling is Good News also because it affirms the resurrection from the dead. The fear of death is perhaps the fundamental fear with which we finite human beings must contend—a fear to which all other apprehensions are directly or indirectly related—a fear that is related to many of the disturbances that bring pastor and people together. Death, with all of its symbols and symptoms—disease, failure, self-sabotage, destructiveness toward others, denial, and other escapist tendencies—is interrelated with most of the traumas that perturb us through our life stages. Like the Good News of reconciliation for the guilty, the Good News of victory over death is intrinsic to the unique context of pastoral care and counseling. In fact, it is to the ill, the dying, and the bereaved that pastoral *care* is the primary ministry.

Affirm Life, Prepare for Death

At least in some parts of the early church it was the custom for the elders of a congregation to anoint the sick with oil as they prayed for their recovery (James 5:14-15). While oil was a medicine for some illnesses, its use in this religious rite was symbolic. In the evolution of the centuries this practice became the sacrament of the Holy Unction or Last Rites in the Roman Catholic Church, in which the anointing became a preparation for death. Other churches have continued to use the rite as a symbol for healing—particularly in Eastern Orthodox, Anglican, and Episcopal Churches. The Roman Catholic Church is now once again using anointing in the ministry of healing.

This shift of anointing with oil from an intercession for healing to a preparation for death and now again to an intercession for healing reflects the dialectical nature of the Christian ministry in illness and health. On the one hand, it is a ministry that affirms life, and therefore, health and healing; on the other hand, it is a ministry that prepares for death.

Many factors are involved in the determination of whether one is healed or dies. Some of the basic of these are attitudes. Attitudes that focus in the denial of reality, or in defeat when facing it, are on the side of death, while attitudes that deal with reality in the vision of hope are on the side of life. Our ministry is to support—to reenforce—the healing processes in human life. Yet this ministry also encompasses the reality of death and therefore accepts death as a possibility in any particular illness and as an ultimate inevitability. Those whom Jesus healed —and these appear to be all who asked and had faith to receive —and even those raised from the dead—ultimately died. Preparation for this inevitability is therefore an indigenous function of the church's ministry. To let God be God in our ministry of intercession means that we reenforce through our pastoral relationships the inherent potential for healing with which God has endowed us, and at the same time we remain open to the possibility of death as the eventual experience of all of God's creatures.

Protest of Death

The human response to this inevitability of death has been universally a protest. Yet death is not the sort of injustice that any protest march can alter. So we either adapt to it and the capricious way it operates, or ignore it as long as we can. The latter is difficult to do because death occurs all around us. Every time someone we know dies, we are reminded that our own time is coming. Yet we can ignore or deny it much longer than in former ages. It is not unusual for one of my students at age 25 to say that he has never attended a funeral. Medical progress has radically reduced childhood deaths and raised the average life span into the seventies.

Death is also difficult to ignore because we fear it. It need not be a destructive fear, however, for it can stimulate us to value the life we have—"to number our days that we may get a heart of wisdom" (Ps. 90:12). The gospel of Christ's resurrection does not eliminate the fear of death. Rather, it gives us a positive support to live with it—the reenforcement we need for the great "leap of faith." But death is not all that we fear: we also fear dying. An "ideal" death is usually one in which an elderly person in relatively good health dies in sleep, thereby avoiding lingering incapacitation and suffering. Tragic and untimely deaths—deaths that include great suffering—are those most feared and resented. Dr. W. Fred Graham suggests that the current interest in running is stimulated in part by the hope that in running regularly one will avoid the debilitating effects of aging—"the terminal helplessness of the dying."

While we resent and fear death, we are also fascinated by it —particularly by violent death. The violence of war, of street crime, of crimes of passion is a popular subject for our novels, our movies, and our television dramas. This same contrast is reflected in the universal desire to survive—to fight for life— and in the death wish that may overtake us in moments of frustration, failure, and depression. Survival has little priority for a suicidal person. Physicians count on a "will to live" in their patients to assist their treatment; they fear a "will to die" in their patients, or even a premonition of death.

This variety in the human response to death is reflected in

the experiences of the dying process as described by Elisabeth Kübler-Ross. These experiences are denial, resentment, bargaining, depression, and acceptance. There is no inevitable progression in these experiences, and their order is not necessarily chronological. Rather one may fluctuate from one to another. Yet the experiences themselves are sufficiently common to be identified. When denial is not effective, the dying person may experience resentment over what is happening. One may also find oneself bargaining—often with God—for recovery. Depression can overwhelm the dying again and again. Through it all there may also emerge the experience of acceptance—now and then—here and there.

Kübler-Ross's book, *On Death and Dying,* has done much to bring death out of the closet to where we can talk about it, and, as she has done, study the process of dying. Another monumental work in this area, *Denial of Death* by Ernest Becker, has also contributed to a growing change in the facing of death. At the time he wrote the book, 1973, Becker was convinced that the denial of death was a major characteristic of our culture and the source of many of its distortions. The response to both Kübler-Ross and Becker (he was awarded the Pulitzer Prize for nonfiction) indicated that this culture was ready for a change.

Kübler-Ross herself has changed. In *Death and Dying,* the only reference to eternal life was a reference to it as an escape from facing the finality of death. Since then she has made more than an about-face and claims now to *know* that eternal life is a reality. She is part of a movement to affirm life after death on the basis of the experiences of those who have "died" and have returned.

What Raymond Moody and others describe as "Life after Life," is not the same as the Good News of the resurrection. Those who have "come back"—have they really been dead? Or is this beatific vision of life after death experienced in what appears to be a state of death but actually is still a state of life?

Other researchers have discovered that some people have very negative experiences during this state. At any rate "scientific findings" about life after death are not really pertinent to the Christian gospel. As Joseph Sitler put it, "If the Church is going to say, 'I believe,' then it must not try to say, 'I believe, but I will believe better if someone will show me the real dope.'" The first editor of the Christian Century, Charles Clayton Morrison, wrote in an Easter editorial, "The early church grew from eleven men to tens of thousands in the first generation after Christ because it conquered death—the final enemy of every living soul." It would be better to say that the early church grew because it *believed* it had conquered death. It is something to be believed rather than to be understood or even to be researched in the laboratories of clinical psychology.

Natural and Unnatural

Death is both natural and unnatural. It is natural in that all life ends in death—it *must* if there is to be reproduction. In spite of the fact that death is necessary for life, we human beings deem it a violation of our *human* nature. Dylan Thomas' familiar protest expresses this unnatural side of death: "Do not go gentle into that good night. . . . rage, rage against the dying of the light." On the other hand, prior to penicillin, pneumonia was considered the old people's friend because it ended their lives when further living could be neither productive nor satisfying. Yet older people often express the desire to live, even though supposedly it is time to die. As a child I overheard my aged granduncle say to my aged grandmother as he faced death, "Whenever death comes, it comes too soon."

Although pneumonia took my mother at age 83, in spite of the drugs, others survive to live qualitatively as well as quantitatively. In some instances, there seems to be little purpose for such survival. Hence the advent of the Living Will, in which one requests that no such life-supporting measures be taken to prolong a mere existence.

While we resent death as an unnatural end to a unique existence, some learn to accept its imminence. The manner in which Charles Lindbergh prepared for his death is an example of such acceptance. When he was told he was suffering from terminal lymphatic cancer, Lindbergh decided to fly to Maui in the Hawaiian Islands, where he desired to be buried next to a little church at the seaside. There he planned his burial, including the words on his tombstone: " 'If I take the wings of the morning and dwell in the uttermost parts of the sea . . .' C. A. L."

Some also seem to welcome death. This is most likely when life has been heavily burdened with pain. The "Burma Surgeon," Gordon Seagrave, was heard to say in his last hours, "I've been in so much pain for so long now, there's just no sense in my staying around any longer. So I'm going home, dear Lord, I'm going home." The ancient sufferer, Job, longed for death as the end to his misery. "Oh that I might have my request, and that God would grant my desire; that it would please God to crush me, that he would let loose his hand and cut me off! This would be my consolation" (Job 6:8-10).

When there is a strong sense of identity with one's people and with one's natural habitat, there seems also to be less protest over death. The Anglican bishop in the novel, *I Heard the Owl Call My Name,* observed this correlation among the Kwakiutl Indians of his British Columbia diocese. When one of his young clergy became terminally ill, he assigned him to this Indian parish in the hope that the Indians would help him in facing death. In the year he spent as their pastor, the young cleric began to identify with them and their world. When the time came that he could no longer fulfill his duties, he chose to die with the Indians rather than return to the hospital as previously planned. The naturalness with which the Indians faced death was based on the naturalness of death in the world of the plants and animals in which they lived. Over the centuries they had developed their own tradition to observe its approach. When the young man heard the owl call his name—a symbol of death's imminence—he was ready.

Tribal identity is rare in our Western world. While there are evils inherent in the tribal system and advantages also in modern urbanization, the fact remains that in our urban areas alienation and loneliness seem only to increase with the density of population. Yet even in more corporate forms of living, sickness and death still raise questions concerning individuality. The Book of Job again is an example. Though it was written in the centuries before Christ and concerned one who was part of a strong corporate identity as the people of God, it speaks to the lonely and isolated individual in today's fractured society. In facing the solitude of death, Job in his sufferings fights the individual's battle against traditional values and beliefs with which he can no longer identify.

The fact remains, however, that in societies where alienation and loneliness are widespread, the fear of death is heightened, for death is the most lonely and alienating of human experiences. Sickness and other forms of suffering, including loneliness, are symbols of death. As a chronically ill parishioner once said to me, "When you are sick, you are sick alone." Yet others who have had similar illnesses or other sufferings may help to break into this isolation, since they know what it is like and can demonstrate this knowledge in their empathy. "When you share your pains with others," said a sufferer, "you can tell by the response those who have suffered deeply from those who have not." Death, however, is bereft of any such sharing. When one dies, one dies alone. Job even envied the trees because they had more assurance in death than people. "For there is hope for a tree, if it be cut down, that it will sprout again, and that its shoots will not cease .... But man dies, and is laid low; man breathes his last, and where is me? (14:7-10).

It is to such questions that the Christian hope speaks, for it is a hope that transcends death. "Christ is risen!" But this hope is not isolated from community support. Although the runner may hope to avoid a lingering death, he cannot guarantee it. This uncertainty colors our perspective on aging. W. Fred Graham describes one's options in this quandary. "I can only watch myself carefully until I see the signs and then put an end to my life. Or I can find a community that will allow me to die and help me as I prepare to be with the Lord" ("The Anxiety of the Runner," *The Christian Century,* Aug. 29, 1979, p. 823). The church is obviously the community to serve this purpose, since it is a community of *faith* united around the transcendent. The challenge to the pastoral ministry is to inspire and direct this community so that it fulfills its potential to be a support for the dying in its midst.

Ministry Based on Hope

The pastor's ministry in death is based on the Christian hope of the resurrection. This hope envisions dying in a dialectical context in which death is the end, but also *not* the end. Among professional helpers it is generally conceded that the pastor should care for the dying. Those whose professional orientation is toward healing and the preservation of life—such as physicians—may experience a particular frustration when they are unable to preserve life. In fact, the terminally ill tend to become isolated and even neglected because there is so little that anyone can do to forestall the inevitable, and also because they are grim reminders of what lies ahead for all of us. The chaplain's walk with the condemned as they go to their execution is symbolic of his function in accompanying the dying on their solitary journey as far as one can go.

The patient's attitude toward his approaching death is an important element in the quality of his life. The physician desires to make the dying as comfortable as possible and may appreciate the pastor's help, since the patient's state of mind is critical toward this end. It is also a key factor to any poten-tial the patient has for survival, since the future of the "termi-nally ill" is not absolutely predictable. Actually we are all "terminal," and therefore need to come to some kind of har-monization of life with death in order to be "freed up" to live. The dying are forced by their circumstances to make some sort of response to what is happening to them. Some face it in hope of eternal life; others, with bitterness over a life that is denied to them. Some deny its reality in spite of the evidence; others look to it as a release from their burdens. Still others accept it stoically as the common lot of humanity.

With the advances in medical science it is difficult to die with a conscious experience of closure. Life-prolonging procedures and heavy dosages of drugs in a sense remove one from one's own death. Particularly the elderly often end their days in understaffed hospitals, feeling neglected and even resented. As their stays are prolonged, their signal lights may be answered only after they have soiled their beds, and their complaints are met with increasing curtness. It is bad enough for the elderly to end their days so completely dependent upon strangers, but when they feel unwanted and uncared for in addition, it is degrading. In her final illness in the hospital, my mother made the rueful comment that older people are acceptable as long as they keep smiling. Death may have come to them sooner, except that they are often kept alive by modern medical means, though there is little reason for them to continue to live. Their alertness fades, and by the time the elderly finally expire, their family and friends are exhausted by the "home-to-hospital" ordeal.

The hospice movement is working to change this way of dying by making the hospital as home-like as possible, and by controlling the intake of drugs so that one may remain involved with life as long as possible. Some community health services are making it possible for the terminally ill who desire it to die at home. These trends toward improving the atmosphere for dying are a welcome advance in humaneness and are a distinct asset to pastors in their ministry to the dying.

Albert Camus' *The Stranger* is an illustration of how one's attitude toward death is connected with one's attitude toward life. Although he was on death row, the Stranger was indifferent toward his approaching execution. When the ministering priest assumed he had fears about his imminent death, the Stranger physically evicted him from his cell. But the Stranger had long been an enigma to others because of his indifference toward *life*. So repressed were his feelings that the only spirited activity of which he seemed capable was an occasional and unpredictable act of violence. For one so estranged from his own being, life's ending was as meaningless as life itself.

Normally, however, one fears one's own death, even though the life that is ending has been devoid of meaning. Though the desire to end one's life is not uncommon, the desire to survive is the more prevalent trend. Death is not only the event that ends one's life; it is a syndrome of events that are directly or indirectly connected with death. All limitings, undesired endings, declinings, are reflections of the final end: sickness, failure, loss, defeat, disintegration. The shadow of death is implicit in these disappointments and diseases, raising the specter of estrangement and abandonment.

The fear that results is essentially the fear of loneliness—alienation. In his *Markings,* Dag Hammarskjold writes, "The anguish of loneliness brings blasts from the storm center of death." A counselee related a dream that was a symbol for this anguish. "I dreamt I was whirling in space—like an ejected piece of matter—whirling further and forever into an endless nothing." The fear of *nothing* is much more difficult to cope with than the fear of something. The concept of nonbeing captures the terror of this perpetual isolation. It is a fear long associated with hell. Though the fear of hell appears considerably reduced in our day, the fear of death seems to contain all of its anguish. Accompanying this anguish is the familiar low self-image, which indicates that the fear of judgment is also still with us. In a society in which people are isolated from one another, death as the final victory of Nothing or Nonbeing, is as frightening as hellfire.

In his or her pastoral care of the dying, the pastor offers the support one needs for the "leap of faith" into *something*. The hope of the resurrection is described in the burial service of my own church as a "sure and certain hope." Such descriptive adjectives for hope would seem to be a contradition in terms. The words, *sure* and *certain,* in our Western ears sound like synonyms for factual and verified. They apply, of course, to a different kind of certainty, for as Paul says, "Hope that is seen is not hope" (Rom. 8:24). This is the certainty of "faith"— another apparent contradiction in terms—as contrasted with the certainty of "sight." It is the certainty that comes from trusting in God. "We may not grasp anything in our uncertainty," says Tillich in *The New Being,* "but that we are grasped by something ultimate, which keeps us in its grasp and from which we may strive in vain to escape, remains absolutely certain."

The pastor accompanies one with this "sure and certain hope" as far as he or she can on what is finally a solitary journey. The pastor's symbolic role as the "bearer of this hope," can be a mixed blessing, however. The early Eldridge Cleaver saw the prison chaplain, for example, as bearing the ineradicable stigma of the establishment that is executing the prisoner or symbolically taking his life through confinement. Pastors do not have to be prison chaplains to represent an oppressive establishment, since the State can take from us only what will be taken anyway sooner or later. It is God himself with whom we have our major misgivings over the inevitability of our own death. An Indian chief, sentenced to death by a U.S. Army court, was being comforted by an army chaplain on his way to the gallows with assurance that life in heaven was far more wonderful than life on earth. "Do you really believe that?" asked the chief.

"Yes, I do," said the chaplain.

"Then change places with me," said the chief, "because I like it here."

Yet in spite of his or her "compromise position" in representing God and of the precarious nature of a "sure and certain hope" in the resurrection, the pastor's ministry in death is nonetheless appreciated. It is a risky responsibility that one assumes on behalf of others. Sociologist Peter Berger acknowledged and appreciated this risk when he gave the following counsel to a youth asking his advice concerning whether he should study for the ministry: "It is persons such as you who show promise of becoming what I hope to find when I go into a church—ministers who know fully the tenuousness of their performance and who yet find it in themselves to carry it on, and to do so on my behalf" ("Letter on the Parish Ministry," *The Christian Century,* April 29, 1964, p. 550). Because the pastor shares in the human fear and protest of death, and because he may be painfully aware of the "tenuousness of his performance," the pastor to the dying needs to come to terms with these doubts and fears within his own soul in order to "find it in himself" to carry on this ministry.

Cancer—A Symbol of Death

We can scarcely discuss pastoral care of the dying in our time without discussing cancer, which has become the disease most associated with death. The experiences of the dying as described by Kübler-Ross—denial and isolation, anger, bargaining, depression, acceptance and hope—are primarily taken from her care of cancer patients. They may, therefore, not be representative of the way people face death in other contexts. The elderly, for example, may face death differently. Where these experiences do apply, however, people may manifest all of them in a single day or may "retrogress" as well as "progress" in the daily battle to affirm their hope. A study of patients with heart disease reveals a pattern of reaction that is somewhat similar to that of the cancer patient. The experiences or phases of this pattern are: terror, expressions of benevolence, reliving the attack, accounting for past achievements, swift mood changes, reconstructing a new life-style, a sense of euphoria.

Despite some similarities in reaction, the attitude toward cancer is more foreboding than that toward heart disease, probably because death by cancer often brings with it the signs of deterioration, the slow "going out" of life. At any rate the mental attitude that people often have toward cancer is itself an obstacle to life and healing since it focuses on hopelessness. I listened while an experienced pastor talked with the wife of a cancer patient who kept referring to her husband as terminal. Finally the pastor said, "Only busses are terminal!" Human beings are also, but he was trying to break her fixation on death so that she might at least be open to the possibility of healing. By prolonging one's focus on the morbid shadows of death, the specter of cancer brings out the Jobian protest in the human spirit.

Job experienced many symptoms of the death syndrome before his physical deterioration convinced him that he was dying. He had lost his wealth, his social position, and his ten children, and he held God accountable. He was not the sort of dying parishioner who would please his pastor by "how well he was taking it." "Thy hands fashioned and made me," he lashed out at God, "and now thou dost turn about and destroy me" (10:8). Providence is a mockery! Seven years before Kübler-Ross published her findings, Granger Westberg in *Good Grief* described remarkably similar experiences of those grieving over the loss of a loved one. One of these is hostility and resentment. The similarity of reaction to dying and to grieving should not be surprising, since the dying are in grief over a loss the magnitude of which is one's own life. In my class in the ministry of dying, I had the opportunity to have as guest teacher an articulate woman who was dying. When she was asked concerning the sorrow of her husband and small children in losing her, she said, "Yes, I feel for them, but I feel more for myself. They are losing one person, a mother, a wife, but I am losing *all* of them."

It is not easy to listen to the Jobian protest. As the symbol bearer of religion, the pastor is the front runner for this kind of assault. Few of us like to be attacked personally or to be put into the position of defending God when he is attacked. Most of us have our own anxieties about death and are not eager to stir them up. There are ways of "listening" to a person's apprehensions or bitterness over death without really focusing on either. The following pastoral visit is an illustration of such avoidance. The person in question was hospitalized for surgery. In previous visits he said little about the nature of this surgery, although when he did mention it, he obliquely indicated a concern.

PASTOR: How are things going this evening, Mr. A?

PATIENT *(somewhat dejected)*: Well, I'm still here.

PASTOR *(evading the dejection)*: Have you found out when you will be able to leave?

PATIENT: No. The doctor was here this morning. He said that they're waiting for a report on the samples they sent to the laboratory.
(He appeared uncomfortable in talking about this.)

PASTOR *(evading the discomfort)*: So you're just waiting.

PATIENT: That's about it. I don't know too much about it. I guess they're trying to find out whether they can dissolve the rest of them with medicine or whether they will have to operate again.
(He persistently referred to his illness in such vague terms.)

PASTOR *(seeking distractive facts)*: Are you able to be up and around?

PATIENT: Well, I tried that yesterday and they said I wasn't supposed to get up. The doctor said I was supposed to stay in bed and rest.

PASTOR *(staying in the "safe zone")*: I suppose you have to be a little careful after such an operation.

PATIENT: Yes, I guess so. I didn't realize there was so much of this type of thing around until I got it.

PASTOR *(evading "this thing")*: We don't always realize what other people go through until we experience it ourselves.

PATIENT: I guess it's just one of those things we can't do anything about.

PASTOR *(trying to stay safely with subject)*: You say they're waiting for a report?

PATIENT: Yes. I don't know exactly what it is. My wife talked to the doctor for quite a while this morning. They were out in the hall.

PASTOR *(avoiding the implication of secrecy)*: Were you able to visit with her today?

PATIENT: Oh, yes. I've had quite a few visitors. *(Pause)* I wish I were out of here *(spoken quietly with a note of despair)*.

PASTOR *(evading the despair)*: It's quite difficult to sit around and wait.

PATIENT: Yes, it is. But I guess that's the way it is. *(Pause)* I suppose I'm a little bitter.

PASTOR: How is that?

PATIENT: Well — I've always been concerned about things like this. I've always taken a thorough physical checkup every year. What good does it do!

PASTOR *(avoiding the protest)*: Are you referring to the surgery?

PATIENT: Yes—and whatever else might still have to be done. *(Pause)* I don't smoke. I've tried to

watch my diet. I guess I'm wondering where's
the fairness of it all!

PASTOR: I see. *(Arising and approaching the bed)*
Well, Mr. A., I have to be on my way. I wonder if you would join me in Scripture and
prayer?

PATIENT: Surely.

The pastor read portions of Psalm 31 and then prayed, expressing thanks for the care the patient was receiving, asking
for guidance for those who were caring for him, and affirming
faith that God is always with us, even in our times of tribula-
tion as we turn to him. The prayer reflected the same "distance"
as the visit.

In commenting on the visit the pastor said:

> My conversation did not help him greatly. I attribute
> this to my own lack of courage. I knew what type of
> operation he had had, and I knew there might be some
> question of cancer. I anticipated this situation before I
> entered the room, and I had become anxious. I think I
> was afraid he really would pour out his fears to me and
> I wouldn't know what to do.

> I believe all of this is connected with my fear of cancer.
> I have experienced death in my family and among close
> friends because of cancer. I often wonder how I would
> react to its death sentence. I have not been able fully to
> resolve this conflict and therefore am inhibited in help-
> ing others deal with it.

The candid way in which the pastor evaluated his ministry
in this instance led to a self-examination that predisposed him
to be less defensive on his next visit.

PATIENT *(dejectedly)*: It looks like I'm going to need
further treatments.

PASTOR: That's disappointing to you.

PATIENT: Yes—but what can you do about it? You have to trust them, I guess.

PASTOR: From what you said the last time I don't suppose that will be easy.

PATIENT: No, it won't. I don't believe it should have gotten this far.

PASTOR: By *it* you mean . . . ?

PATIENT: This ah, ah—malignancy.

PASTOR: As you said last time, it doesn't seem fair to you.

PATIENT: No, but here it is anyhow.

PASTOR: You have the malignancy—and what does that mean in your mind?

PATIENT: I guess it means—I may not get better.

PASTOR: That you'll die?

PATIENT: Yes—and I'm not ready for that at all. I want to live!

The visit continued in this sharing manner and led, like the former visit, to prayer. But the petitions this time were far more personal and specific.

If a Man Die—Shall He Live Again?

One's fears and protests need to be expressed and accepted rather than stifled. Yet behind the Jobian protest there is also the Jobian question, "If a man die, shall he live again?" In a Christian ministry to the dying this question needs to be confronted. In my first ministry to a dying person as a parish pastor I found myself with an elderly man who calmly faced the reality of his imminent death. After administering the sacrament of the Holy Communion to him, which had been requested, I considered it my role to assure him that in dying he would be with the Lord. I suppose I thought that my saying this as a pastor would reenforce him in his faith. I was shaken out of my naivete by his candid response. "You may be right,

Reverend," he said, "but I'll tell you something—I'll soon find out!"

The question, "If a man die, shall he live again?" continues to challenge us. In our scientific orientation we want to *know* and not just to *believe*. The noted parapsychologist, J. B. Rhine, has exemplified this quest. Enrolled at a church college with the intention of entering the ministry, he lost his religion in his psychology class. Since his beginning days as Director of the Duke University Parapsychology Laboratory, he has attempted to recover by the scientific method his belief in the spiritual nature of humanity. He has become convinced that his work in parapsychology has sustained the "soul theory of man by empirical research." Regarding the survival of death he says, "In the light of scientific research some form of survival is a possibility."

If a man die, shall he live again? Though Rhine says that scientifically it is a possibility, he also states, "It is becoming increasingly clear that a scientific decision is not even within sight from our present position." Obviously this question is not settled like other questions—scientifically, clinically, legally. We still wrestle with it in loneliness, as have those before us. There are other questions also that we cannot answer, such as those implicit in the Jobian protest: why tragedy? why untimely deaths? We can affirm ourselves in such questions only by a "leap of faith," and as we confront our own death, we approach the leap of faith in its ultimate dimension. Though it is a lonely leap, there is a vital role to those who are facing it for the pastoral ministry with its historic tradition of faith.

With a Reasonable Hope

The dying person is confronted by the ultimate leap in faith only if he is aware of his probable death. This brings up the old question, still with us, concerning whether one should be told the truth about his condition. Some continue to argue that certain patients do not want to know. What is frequently overlooked in this debate is that professional helpers, including physicians, may have their own personal hangups on facing death, and subconsciously are looking for a justification for avoiding the confrontation. This fact, of course, highly colors one's ability to determine how much the patient wants to know or is able to bear.

Dr. Robert Staehlen of the Anderson Cancer Clinic at the Texas Medical Center advocates the practice of telling the truth in a way that the patient can understand, and always within the context of a realistic hope. He maintains that there is always something to which the physician can point positively in the patient's condition, either in what he plans to do for the patient's potential or limited recovery, or for arresting the disease, or of extending the patient's usefulness for productive living for whatever time he has remaining. It is his position that any procedure that combines honesty with hope is in the interest of both ethics and therapy. After such a conference with a patient, Staehlen says, he is often followed by the patient's relatives seeking to know what really is the truth. "I've already given it to you," he says. "Now you better get back before the patient surmises otherwise." He thus prevents the furtive conference away from the patient that stimulates his negative imagination, as was the case in the pastoral visit previously noted. When physicians and pastors are cooperative, the pastor may be present when the physician informs the patient of his or her condition, or may follow the physician's conference with a pastoral visit.

The principle of honesty accompanied by hope is a good procedure for the pastor also to follow as he or she assists the dying person in the transition from an awareness to an acceptance of the situation. Together they can enter the valley of the shadow of death, characterized by depression and discouragement, to the renewed hope of dwelling in the house of the Lord forever—again and again in the fluctuations that characterize those enduring the pain of loss. The same is true for the pastor's ministry to the bereaved. It is a long and arduous route from the death of a loved one to a genuine involvement in life again.

The Christian faith is grounded in hope. Faith is based not only on what God has done or is doing, but also on what he *will* do. The fullness is yet to come. The promises of God are a basis for whatever mission the church has in the world. While these promises go beyond the individual believer, they also include him or her. As Jürgen Moltmann puts it, "Creative love finds the comprehensive future in view of which it lives" in the hope of the resurrection.

In this perspective death is paradoxically the prelude to new life. Even as the old must die to make room for the new in the world of nature, so in the world of the spirit the old nature dies so that the new nature can come forth, again and again. While the body after reaching its maturation in growth begins its slow but ultimately relentless aging process toward its consummation in death, the spirit through its death and resurrection process is directed toward life. The Christian approach to quality living is based on this continuous renewal of the human spirit, though the "outer nature is wasting away" (2 Cor. 4:16).

This is the hope not only for the dying but for all of us. In the midst of life, death is present. Those who are seriously ill are not different in kind from those who are well, but rather in degree. The aging process and the death syndrome are the common lot. Those who are seriously ill, however, differ from those who are well in that their condition brings into sharp relief their finitude. Those facing death have an existential insight into the value of quality living. A colleague of mine in a neighboring seminary, Thomas Campbell, poignantly expressed this awareness as he was dying of cancer. "I have been grasped by God's graciousness during these months in ways which cannot possibly be put into words, but certainly I can and must point toward them. I have learned that Christian hope is at least as rich and variegated in meaning as Christian love. . . . The gift I have found is that a deeper sense of *kairos* (especially urgent and fulfilling *time*) makes one much less agitated about battles lost, results less than one had hoped for, and people who do not see things the way you do. I have been able to grant more 'freedom' both to myself *and* to others."

The pastoral ministry to the dying is thus a renewal ministry. Obviously it is to the advantage of this ministry that the person is aware of his condition. The integrating hope is for the new creation in Christ Jesus. Those who are aware of their approaching death have a greater clarity regarding specific values in life—values which inevitably focus on our relationships. The latter days are often marked by a greater appreciation of personal intimacies. When hope regarding the *quantity* of life is limited by medical prognosis, hope for its *quality* may increase.

In ministering to Job, his fourth counselor, Elihu, said he would answer Job's question, namely, how was he any better off than if he had lived a sinful life? While anybody who is in dire straits may call on God for relief, Elihu said, Job as a person covenanted to God was in a position to pray for more, namely for "songs in the night." *Song* is the symbol for joy, and *night,* the symbol for distress. To have joy in the midst of distress, light in the midst of darkness, songs in the midst of night, is the believer's potential. The ancient counselor's insight contains the scope of the pastor's ministry to sufferers.

In 1973 Orville Kelley, ill with terminal cancer, held a conference with his three young children. Since his awareness of his disease, things had not been going well at home. Kelley was depressed, and the others were on edge not knowing what to say. "I want you three to help me live with this cancer," he said. "There will be bad days for us, but we can have good days too. We don't have to like death, but we don't have to be terrified by it either." This was the beginning of Make Today Count, an organization founded by Kelley for the terminally ill and their families. The quality of life in his family was remarkably changed, and after Kelley wrote about it in a Burlington, Iowa, newspaper, he received the inquiries that ultimately led to the organization.

At this writing—six years later—Kelley is still living, making speeches about what dying has done for him and his family in "making today count." His experience indicates that quality of life may have some effect on quantity of life. When one has a meaning and purpose for living, when his spirit is nurtured in intimate supportive relationships, his physical health, including his resistance to disease, is positively affected.

According to research in the area, our personality predispositions may predispose us to specific diseases of the body. Cancer patients, for example, tend to be controlled persons, secretive by nature, who "hold it all in." Heart patients, on the other hand, tend to be hard-driving perfectionists with a high level of stress. These "findings" reveal nothing more than trends and may be inapplicable to specific patients. Even if the personality factor is applicable, it is only one factor among an unknown number of those that may expose one to the disease. However, given the trend, the quality of living that is often experienced by the dying and their families could be in the emancipation from these personality predispositions that have previously inhibited one's personal growth.

Ministry to the dying, therefore, focuses on assisting the patient to share more fully with us and through us with God, and thus to participate more fully in the reconciliation that is ours through Christ. Because the anticipation of death brings to all concerned a sharp reorganization in one's hierarchy of values, the deepening of family or other intimate relationships is the frequent by-product of an approach that combines honesty with a realistic hope. Not the least of these relationships to grow in intimacy is one's relationship with God. When Job

finally received his songs in the night, he said, "I had heard of
thee [God] by the hearing of the ear, but now my eye sees
thee" (42:5).

Sharing the Hope of Eternal Life

In this milieu of sharing among patient, pastor, family, and
friends, the hope of eternal life can also be shared. Dependent
as it is upon the leap of faith, the resurrection hope is fundamental to any Christian approach to death. The centrality of
Easter in the Christian calendar is not due simply to the centrality of the resurrection in the Christ-event, but also to the
centrality of the hope that the Christ-event brings to the believer. "Because I live, you shall live also" (John 14:19). The
believer participates in the Good News that Christ is the first
fruits of a great harvest to follow. His resurrection is the
breakthrough of the light of life into the darkness of death.
Death is now the *conquered* enemy.

The hope of eternal life is a positive influence upon the
health of the patient. It does not weaken his will to live, as
might superficially be supposed. Rather it is life-encouraging.
In contrast to the disintegration that characterizes despair,
hope, as despair's opposite, is by its very definition a focus for
integration. While despair and resignation may extend their
negativity into bodily functions, hope is health-oriented. The
hope of eternal life is no exception. Rather it may have an
even greater positive effect because of its specific application to
the fear of death, and because it is combined with an equally
positive influence—trust in God. It is this trust that makes the
difference between acceptance of death and resignation to it.

A patient who was aware of the critical nature of her illness,
said to her pastor, "When I was being X-rayed this morning, I
folded my hands and told the Lord that I was ready either way.
I want to live, but I am also ready to die."

As the pastor listened to her, he said, "What keeps running through my mind as you speak are the words from the New Testament, 'Whether we live or whether we die, we are the Lord's.'"

"That says it," said the patient. "I'm with *him* either way."

The Christian hope is not simply a hope for some*thing* but for some*one*. Hope identifies us with Christ. While we cannot envision to any degree of clarity what the fulfillment of life will be like, "we know that when he appears, we shall be like him, for we shall see him as he is" (1 John 3:2). "Now I know in part; then I shall understand fully, even as I have been fully understood" (1 Cor. 13:12). Hope as anticipation is an attribute of strength, not of weakness.

The Good News contains also the news of God's good promises. These promises are inherent in the covenant relationship that we, as the people of God, have with God, a covenant sealed by the sacramental rite of Baptism, in which our identification with Christ is symbolically expressed. Being baptized is being baptized into Christ; it is putting on Christ and being joined—buried—with him in death, that as he has risen from the dead, we too shall live in newness of life. This existential identification with Christ in his death and resurrection is an experience realizable in the present in terms of new life in the spirit, of *quality* of life. It extends also into the future in the hope for the resurrection of the dead.

No limits are placed on the quality of fulfillment associated with this hope. St. Paul's familiar comparison between *now* and *then* is particularly applicable to the sufferings of the dying. "I consider the sufferings of this present time are not worth comparing with the glory that is to be revealed in us" (Rom. 8:18). And again, "What no eye has seen, nor ear heard, nor the heart of man conceived, what God has prepared for those who love him" (1 Cor. 2:9).

Though it takes a leap of faith to transcend the limits of life as we know it, the hope of eternal life is still a realistic hope.

In matters that go beyond the boundaries of empirical science —and these include the meaning and purpose of life—our reason functions on the basis of presuppositions that are related to the realm of faith. These presuppositions are not opposed by science since they are in a different realm. Our faith comes out of our personal experiences, and these are closely associated with our personal relationships.

For the dying person the time that remains is potentially a time for the deepening of these relationships. Life as we know it and life as we anticipate it are connected by the perspective of faith. Realized and future-oriented foci in eschatology are united in our new nature in Christ whose anticipations penetrate the boundary of death. "Neither death, nor life . . . nor things present, nor things to come . . . nor anything else in all creation will be able to separate us from the love of God in Christ Jesus our Lord" (Rom. 8:38-39).

Within the framework of hope the truth can be shared not only openly but positively. The truth about the patient's condition does not imply any certainty about one's imminent demise except where specific vital organs have ceased to function, as is the case in some severely burned persons. There are usually too many possible factors, including the power of faith and of intercessory prayer, for any predictive certainty over how long one has yet to live. The patient's hope for eternal life, therefore, is not unrelated to the hope of others of the Christian fellowship who are momentarily well, since the terminus of their health is also uncertain.

Death is the human being's grand finale, one's "end of the line," but not one's destination. Death is the enemy of humanity, but Christ has overcome it. On the one hand, we are participants in the world of nature and under nature's laws, and on the other hand, we are children of God and under the promises of God. The two worlds are united by faith in the one God who is Lord of heaven and earth.

Summary

The Good News of victory over death is an affirmation of life in every facet of the human experience. It is a protest of death and all of its influences that distort and destroy life. Though death is inherent in the natural order of things, it is unnatural in its apparent destruction of the "eternity" that God has "put into man's mind" (Eccles. 3:11). Estrangement and loneliness, symbols of death that abound in our day, tend to intensify the fear of death. The Good News puts hope into our minds. The pastoral care of the dying protects a person's right to entertain this hope in an atmosphere of human dignity and support. The quality of life is as much or more of a pastoral concern as the quantity.

The hope of eternal life is supported by a continuous ministry of Christian fellowship, as those who are members one of another in the body of Christ, minister to each other. We need to surround with the supportive fellowship of the congregation those who are afflicted. This applies to the bereaved as well as the dying. Like the dying, the bereaved are often neglected. In the weeks and months following the death of a loved one, the contacts become fewer and fewer. In a study made at the University of Minnesota concerning the pastoral care of bereaved parents, the major complaint of these parents was that the pastor—as well as the lay members of the congregation—ceased to minister to them on any personal basis shortly after the funeral ("When a Child Dies," by Helen Paulsen MacInnis, *The Christian Century,* Jan. 1979). Actually, the loss may seem more grievous three, six, or nine months after the death. Beside ministering to the bereaved during this year of grieving, pastors need to catalyze their lay people to do the same, so that these sufferers have someone with whom to share concerning their memories of the loved one and their pain in the loss.

In this reference to the pastor's catalyzation of lay people to

assist him or her in the pastoral care of the dying, we are assuming the use of resources unique to the pastoral ministry.
Other such resources—God-talk, Scripture, prayer—have also
been assumed in the illustrations used to show the significance
of the specific faith of the pastoral ministry to human needs.
We turn now to these distinctive resources for pastoral care
and counseling, each of which is an expression of the specific
faith delineated in pastoral theology.

5

Faith's Role
in the Counseling Process:
Dialogical Use of God-Talk

A Major Asset

Because of its specific faith, a major asset for pastoral counseling is that pastor and people can dialogue about faith in God, the way of Christ, the discipline of prayer, and divine providence, as an integral part of the therapeutic process. One can do this with a Christian psychotherapist or psychiatrist also, but not because of his or her profession or of the nature of psychotherapy or psychiatry, but only because of the character of the individual therapist. In pastoral counseling such conversation is organic to the counseling structure as it is to pastoral care, being normal to the discipline itself; it does not take place simply because of the individual who is the counselor.

The pastoral counselor is educated in the area of theology and its relationship to human dynamics and in the pastoral use of specifically religious resources for counseling, such as Scripture, meditation and prayer. He or she is often educated also in clinical skills that utilize psychological insights. Since an understanding of psychology is important to pastoral counseling, pastoral theology must include it, even as systematic theology includes the discipline of coherent and rational thought, and exegetical theology includes the science of historical and textual analysis. The psychology involved in pastoral counseling is actually an implication of its theological base, since pastoral theology is focused on ministry. It needs, therefore, to incorporate a knowledge of the dynamics of intrapersonal and interpersonal relationships.

The fact that religious symbols are indigenous to pastoral counseling because of its specific faith does not mean that these symbols are always utilized in pastoral counseling. Pastoral counselors may deliberately refrain from any reference to God-talk in any particular counseling session because they deem it inappropriate. Like other counselors they begin where the counselee is—not where they wish him or her to be. For a particular counselee in a particular moment, the introduction of God-talk may seem a strange interference in communication. It may be misunderstood because of the distorted conception that the counselee projects onto religious symbols due to previously negative conditioning experiences. At the other extreme pastors may abstain from God-talk in pastoral care and counseling in order to discourage what they believe to be a religious facade. Some people misuse religious language to reenforce their evasion of reality. Others misuse it as a way of saying what they believe pastors want to hear. Still others believe that by using religious words they are giving the right impression— "sounding like a Christian."

When religious symbols and resources are not used explicitly in any particular counseling session, the specific faith of pastoral counseling may still be communicated through the person of the pastor—as well as the counselee, in some instances—in the perspective within which he or she views the human scene. It is communicated also in the caring and acceptance that is extended in the counseling relationship. God's grace can be received through nonverbal as well as verbal symbols.

Yet the explicit communication of the specific faith in the dialogical medium is a distinctive asset for pastoral counseling when the circumstances are appropriate. As Carroll Wise has

pointed out in *The Meaning of Pastoral Care,* the psychotherapist, particularly if he or she is analytically oriented, is
concerned about relating to the unconscious mind of the
counselee. When the pastor uses the verbal symbols associated
with the specific faith and communicates the spirit behind
them, he or she may be "speaking more directly and effectively
to the unconscious than the psychotherapist."

Because these religious symbols have been used superficially
in pastoral care, their value can be overlooked. When they are
introduced into the counseling process, this does not necessarily
mean that the pastor and/or counselee are consciously or un-
consciously attempting to evade more difficult areas or tasks,
or that the counseling process is thereby being shunted to a
superficial level. Rather, their introduction can mean that the
dialogue is entering a difficult but significant dimension and
that a productive encounter with basic issues can result.

We need to reaffirm at the outset, however, that in spite of
the indigenous nature of God-talk to pastoral care and counseling, the use of these "religious words" is not the identifying
character of a pastoral encounter. One can have a pastoral encounter without them; one can also use them and not have a
pastoral encounter. That which constitutes the pastoral nature
of an encounter is the attitude—the mind-set, the viewpoint—
that envisions the healing function in terms of faith in God.
It is out of this mind-set that God-talk may become a medium
of expression. When this mental frame of reference *is,* there is
no need to prove it by verbalization. Pastors may feel an unnatural pressure—particularly with a certain type of individual
—to utilize the traditional forms that will identify their role
and hence "justify" them in the other's eyes. When forms are
misused for this purpose, they deny the spirit that they were
meant to convey. It is the perspective itself, and not the specific
words or tonal quality or procedures, that sets the direction
for a pastoral encounter. Traditional forms or religious words
need to come forth naturally—organically—from this basic per-

spective so that there is congruence between them. God is not brought into the encounter when his name is spoken; neither is he absent if his name is not spoken. His presence *is*. Our realization of it depends upon the perspective within which we perceive the present moment.

One of the pioneers in pastoral counseling in its modern form, John Sutherland Bonnell, had an empty chair in his counseling room to remind him of the presence of the Unseen One. This was before Gestalt therapists utilized the empty chair for hypostatizing inner and outer polarities. Bonnell's empty chair reminds me of a placard that hung on the wall above the dinner table of my childhood home: "Christ is the Unseen Guest at every meal, the Silent Listener to every conversation." I believe I was a bit intimidated by this reminder of the Presence, but it *was* a reminder.

If we are not clear on the relationship of God-talk to a pastoral encounter, religious symbols can be misused for all sorts of unworthy ends. It is hard for some of us to resist the pressure to play a role when God-talk enters the dialogue. Should a suffering parishioner, for example, make a positive reference to God or prayer, for whatever reason, the pastor may feel constrained to reenforce this expression by speaking more positively about God or prayer. The following excerpt from a pastoral care visit to a hospitalized parishioner is typical of this tendency. Near the close of the visit, during which the pastor had responded empathically to the needs of the patient, the patient introduced God-talk into the dialogue.

> PATIENT: In spite of my blues—and I surely have been dwelling on them, haven't I?—I really know that God is good, and I can continue to trust him.
>
> PASTOR: Yes—it's nice that we have such a wonderful God in whom we can trust at times like these.

PATIENT: If I couldn't pray, I don't know what I would do.

PASTOR: Yes, prayer is a wonderful thing; it is good we can pray and know that he hears our prayers.

PATIENT: Yes *(silence)*.

PASTOR *(sensing the end of the road in the conversation)*: Shall we have a little word of prayer now?

PATIENT: Yes—please do.

In spite of how well the pastor had responded to the feelings of the patient prior to the introduction of God-talk, the pastor's need to identify with this talk—actually to be the authority in it—proved too much for his good counseling sense to combat. Instead of continuing as a pastoral counselor, he became a competitor with the patient in offering prayer and doxologies to God. Naturally, with his symbolic authority in this area, he easily overwhelmed his parishioner, and the conversation ended. The *dialogue* had, in fact, ended previously. Under the pressure of the subsequent silence, he obviously felt that the only way out was to do what he had been eulogizing, thus putting the traditional finale to the visit. An unfortunate by-product of this kind of response to God-talk is that the pastor was clearly informing the parishioner of what he wanted to hear, which in turn exerts a subtle pressure on her to say what is pleasing. In fact, in this instance, the patient may have expressed her faith to some extent because she felt guilty about being so negative. To rectify the imbalance—perhaps even to give a "better" impression—she may have added her qualifying comment. Of course, this is a conjecture, but a conjecture that pastors need to keep in mind. Studies show that counselees tend to adapt to what they believe is the conceptual mind-set of the counselor—speaking in psychological terms with a psychologist, in medical terms with a physician, and in religious terms with a pastor.

The dialogical challenge is to assist the person to express what he or she *means* by the terms. In the above instance the pastor might have encouraged the patient to share more fully how her faith had been helpful. He could have preserved the dialogical milieu had he responded to her profession of faith with interest rather than with role-expectancy.

> PATIENT: In spite of my blues—and I surely have been dwelling on them, haven't I?—I really know that God is good, and I can continue to trust him.
>
> PASTOR: You sound like you are speaking from experience.

There is the possibility that this response might encourage the patient to share more specifically about her life with God.

The authority role that the pastor may feel obligated to assume when God-talk is injected into the dialogue tends to be phony. At these times he can sound like he and God have a special connection. The implication is that he is of a different breed from others, when actually he has a similar struggle with doubt. No wonder, then, that he brings dialogue to an end. It is hard to dialogue with one who "has it all together."

In contrast to the above pastor's use of God-talk—and perhaps also the parishioner's—is that of the Old Testament sufferer, Job. God-talk for him was the only way he could conceptualize and express the deep conflict he was experiencing. Had he, or those counseling with him, avoided God-talk, the dialogue would have been seriously limited so far as his needs were concerned. God was at the center, not the periphery, of his problem. God-talk offered him the symbols capable of communicating his irreducible conflict over meaning and purpose.

Job's conflict is an example of Viktor Frankl's emphasis in logotherapy that the need for meaning is at the center of human functioning. His conflict was over the *logos*—the Word, the commitment, the meaning to life in which he had trusted, but which now seemed to have betrayed him. The Jobian protest is inescapably God-centered. His question is to the point, "If it is not he, who then is it?" (Job 9:24). If God (Providence) is not in charge, who or what is? If he is, he is accountable. This seems to be the way the sufferer is prone to reason—today, as well as in Old Testament times—providing he or she and the pastor can tolerate the despair that comes to the fore in such soul searching.

Pastors encounter the Jobian protest from their parishioners as they visit in hospitals and in bereaved homes and as they involve themselves in the personal, marital, and family problems of the people. A most intense expression of this protest came from a patient in a rehabilitation center who was suffering from a paralyzing accident. Pointing to the hospital files, he said to his pastor, "Look at all those files! All those records in those files are nothing. That's what they are—nothing! Only names of people, people who are no longer people, but only like me. Do you know what I am saying? Can you read my feelings? Do you know what I mean?"

The pastor tried to put into words his empathy. "I suppose you mean that there is nothing left for you, everything is gone: home, family, love, all are gone."

Knowing he had been understood, the sufferer was encouraged to continue. "Yes, nothing is left. All the doctors can do is give advice and talk. But it doesn't help. I am still me, and every day is just the same. There just isn't any answer. Everything here at the hospital is so neat and clean, but what difference does it make? Nobody has the answers. Jesus Christ didn't have the answers. There are no answers." At this point he broke down and clutched the pastor's hand so hard that it was uncomfortable.

Although he used it negatively, in naming the name of Christ, the sufferer was giving expression to the heart of his problem. It is precisely this experience at the community level that led Rabbi Richard Rubenstein to write *After Auschwitz.*

According to Rubenstein, any God who would allow six million of his chosen people to go to the gas ovens is dead. Religion, henceforth, will have to get along without him. After many years Rubenstein says he still holds his position, although he admits the religious Jewish people—contrary to his anticipations—have continued to affirm their faith in the God of the Old Testament covenant.

Job in his despair doubted the *goodness* of God, while his modern counterparts are more likely to doubt his existence. Camus' *The Stranger* is an illustration of the latter. The Stranger had made his "adjustment" to a meaningless existence. He was detached, indifferent, and concerned only about the satisfactions of immediate sensory experience. He assumed it was obvious that he did not believe in God.

People like the Stranger are hurt persons. Their feelings are too wounded to deal with directly. So they repress them and develop a controlled and detached bearing. Yet there is a protest in this repression. It is the price they pay for stifling much of their vitality. When we cannot take our negative or unpleasant passions, we lose the capacity for positive or pleasant ones. At times it is our physical bodies that take the brunt of the protest. The negative vitality does not disappear because it is repressed; rather it may "attack" our bodies. The compensatory physical ailments then belie the external calm.

It is difficult to find a satisfactory substitute for the role that religion plays in human life. Speaking candidly in his ninety-second year about his Roman Catholic background from which he departed years ago, historian-philosopher Will Durant said, "It is not merely that you long to recover the faith. You know that is impossible. But there is a tremendous vacuum where the faith used to be. And you feel that vacuum."

Even those who have found substitutes for God in their search for meaning may have moments of nostalgic reflection. Jean-Paul Sartre, for example, who took his existential leap into Nothing, said in reflection, "If things had been different,

I might have struck up something with God." Sartre, of course, probably said this with tongue in cheek. Yet, in view of his childhood environment, he had good reason for saying it. A cousin of his, Albert Schweitzer, managed to "strike up something with God" with distinction.

As an observer of American society, Viktor Frankl notes our preoccupation with sex and sees it as a symbol of our search for a *recovery of purpose and meaning.* Sex, says Frankl, has become our substitute for our *loss of spiritual moorings,* and in this capacity serves as an escape from an *existential despair.* So even our cultural preoccupation with sex may take us back to religion and God-talk. One factor at least in this preoccupation is the search for meaning and for intimacy, both of which have deeply spiritual dimensions.

Our concern is for a pertinent use of God-talk in pastoral care and counseling—one that is based on the recognition of a difference between the word-symbol and the conceptualization it may represent in any particular mind. The religious experience of Martin Luther is an example in point. The word *God* for the suffering monk represented a negative mental image that conjured up a great deal of anxiety and hostility. The tower-room experience brought about a change in Luther because it brought about a change in his mental image of God. The word *God* now represented a more positive image, stimulating feelings of security and love. The symbol's meaning was changed without the symbol itself being changed. The man who had once wished he could get rid of God now wished more of him. The God he could not love before was now the God whom he *could* love.

Our purpose as pastoral counselors is to assist people in their movement from a superficial use of God-talk to the encounter with the reality that this language symbolizes. To do this we need to deal with the God-talk symbols contextually—in the milieu of dialogue—rather than from any supposed authority of the pastor in such matters. Jesus is described in the Gospels as one who spoke with authority and not as the scribes. Yet the scribes considered themselves authorities and were so recognized by the people. Their authority, however, was an authority about the sources, the formulas, the traditions. In contrast, Jesus spoke as one who knew from his own involvement. He was secure in being his own source. In matters of faith any authority one has that concerns sources, if not accompanied by the authority of one's own involvement, tends to stifle dialogue. In contrast the authority that comes from one's own involvement with God is by its very nature grounded in a sharing dimension. Therefore it can function within the flexibility that is needed for dialogue.

The Dialogical Structure

Pastoral counseling is dialogical in structure: there is listening and speaking, giving and receiving. Because of the stimulative nature of each contribution to the dialogue, its outcome is unpredictable. It is an experience for the counselor no less than for the counselee. The use of God-talk in pastoral counseling, therefore, needs to be within the dialogical dynamic. This makes its use in pastoral counseling something other than its use in religious education or in preaching. Teaching may take place within the pastoral counseling milieu, but counseling is not primarily teaching. Some hortatory conversation may occur in pastoral counseling, but counseling is not primarily preaching. Unfortunately, the only disciplines which incorporate God-talk into their system are religious education and preaching. The schools of psychotherapy obviously have not been helpful in this regard, as they have in other aspects of pastoral counseling.

The tendency has been for the pastor simply to transfer the structure of teaching or preaching into the counseling when God-talk enters the dialogue. Consequently, the dialogical process involved previously usually comes to an end. Both teaching and preaching can and should have a dialogical dimension, at least in the mind of the teacher or preacher. The opportunity for engaging in any actual dialogue is limited to some extent in the context of teaching, and almost entirely in preaching. In counseling, however, dialogue is at the heart of the medium. There needs, therefore, to be a structure specifically oriented to pastoral counseling for the use of God-talk in the counseling milieu.

The greatest obstacle to dialogue in counseling is defensiveness. When we become defensive, we cease sharing and begin erecting walls. Unfortunately, pastors can become defensive when dealing with God-talk. Without the protection of the pulpit or the teacher's lectern they can feel vulnerable and exposed when dialoguing in God-talk. Perhaps God-talk is too close to our pastoral identity for us to feel at ease in the unpredictable milieu of dialogue. At any rate, when we become defensive, our concentration becomes divided. With one part of our mind we are listening to the counselee, and with the other part we are defending our position. I liken the difference to that between *responding* and *reacting*. In responding, the counselor is drawn toward the counselee in empathic identification. In reacting, one is thrown back on oneself to defend one's vulnerability.

We have seen an example of reacting in the previous verbatim excerpt, when the counselee was ostensibly positive in her use of God-talk. When the counselee is negative, the situation may be particularly threatening. If the counselee is questioning his or her faith or even attacking the tenets of religion, pastors may find it difficult not to feel personally attacked. They may feel impelled to convince the counselee to believe otherwise. Relying on many words when fewer words have seemingly failed, they may "pound home the point," unable to let the matter rest until they achieve some minimal consensus. Like Job's three defensive counselors, pastors may emotionally concentrate on a rational justification of their position in order to evade the emotional threat of disagreement at so sensitive an area.

In Transactional Analysis terms, we pastors tend to become *parental* when engaged in God-talk with our parishioners. In fact Eric Berne sees each of his three ego-states—parent, adult, child—as identified with a particular profession. The child occupation is the circus clown; the adult occupation is his own, the psychiatrist; and the parental occupation is the clergyperson. He has some historic backing for this selection. The clergyperson is called Father in some churches, and some laypersons in most churches display the emotional behavior of children who compete for their parents'—in this case the clergyperson's—favor.

While we pastors may be restive with this occupational identification with the parental ego-state, we may as well face up to the fact that this is the way some people perceive us. Vocationally, we do have a parental function. But we also have the child and adult functions as well. We need the flexibility to respond to situations contextually rather than compulsively. For example, it takes a certain personal and vocational security to deal conversationally with our parishioners in God-talk from the perspective of the adult ego-state. The counselee then is also an adult—not a child—and therefore his or her insights into God-talk have significant dialogical input. Should our insecurity move us into a parental state at this point, we develop what Paul calls "itching ears." We itch to hear what we want to hear. We also develop "screening ears" so that we do not hear what we do not *want* to hear. Either we avoid responding to the threatening issue, or we react by monopolizing the conversation. In either case dialogue is successfully stifled.

Dialogue implies tension, the word deriving from the Greek, *dialogizomai,* which means "to bring together different reasonings." Differences are threatening, even as they are enriching. To avoid the tension of dialogue, both counselor and counselee may be tempted to control conversation by active or passive means. Besides being "two-way," dialogue is a function that cannot be approached with the usual preparation. It centers in involvement. In the early days of psychoanalytic practice the analyst maintained a protective aloofness and disinterested professionalism. He had his counterparts among the clergy. The trend now, however, is in the opposite direction, in which the sharing of feelings and ideas characterizes the therapeutic relationship. (Sidney Jourard was an influential stimulus in this trend with his book, *The Transparent Self*. N.Y.: Van Nostrand Reinhold, rev. ed., 1971.)

In counseling when the subject of the conversation is religion, the pastoral counselor may feel too identified with the subject to be open to conflict, being threatened by the unpredictability of the outcome. One needs to mature to the point where one's own security or ego is not under attack when one's religious position is not being accepted. Then one is liberated to respond to whatever God-talk may indicate in any particular situation. This means, in effect, to let one's adult ego-state take charge. The role of the counselor is normally that directed by the adult ego-state. The counselor may be childlike or parentlike if the needs of the counselee so warrant, but it is as the adult that he or she decides which ego-state is appropriate. This relaxed approach to God-talk may move counselor and counselee from a rigid or superficial use of it—from trying to prove or defend something—to genuine communication at the deep levels of the human spirit.

On meeting the first time with a married couple having difficulties, I was taken aback by the husband's request. "Reverend, I'm here to get help for my marriage, but I don't want any God-stuff. I just don't believe in it." Although I was tempted to ask him why he came to a pastor, I decided against it. This was probably a wise decision at the time since I was impulsively defensive. I could also have informed him that I would not permit myself to be limited in my approach and that he would need to trust that I would not attempt to manipulate him religiously. Instead I accepted him where he was and abstained from God-talk. The next session his wife brought up the subject of grace before meals as a point of contention. Feeling no pressure from me, the husband proceeded to give his own views on the subject and, to my surprise, revealed a religious sensitivity.

As I look back on this experience, I believe I missed an opportunity to "draw out" this man in a potentially significant area of his life. *Why* was he so resistant to God-talk? Had I not been so concerned about sounding defensive or so "hung up" on the supposed need to give an immediate answer to every question, I might have simply responded to what he was communicating: "I'm interested in that request. You evidently have had some negative experiences with religion." His response could have opened a door into his life that would be helpful in throwing light on the roots of his present state of mind. We may have had a significant dialogue in the negative use of religion in his development which would have given me an opportunity to make a more intelligent response to his request. In the meantime rapport would have been initiated, of which I had little at the beginning, and this would be a growing asset in maximizing the dialogical potential of the moment.

Verbatim Analysis

As an illustration of the dialogical approach to the use of God-talk, we shall analyze in detail a verbatim report of a counseling session—the fourth visit by a pastor with a seventeen-year-old resident of a state reformatory. Unlike many residents in correctional institutions, the counselee came from an unbroken home in which both parents attended church regularly. The young man himself, however, had become inactive in the church during his adolescence. The recorded dialogue centers on the religious dimension of guilt following the pas-

tor's use of God-talk when there seemed to be a natural opening. After introducing the God-talk, however, the pastor
"changed gears" as the dialogue became threatening to him,
since the counseling approach is quite different before and after
the introduction of God-talk. As a result, the nature of the
counselee's involvement also changed.

P 1: Well, Bob, how have you been this past week?

R 1: Oh, pretty good, I guess I'm getting used to this
place. Anyway it doesn't bother me as much as
it did at first to think about where I actually am.

P 2: I see, then you feel more relaxed now.

R 2: Yes, I guess that's part of it. I've also been able to
think more about what I've done and all the mis-
takes I made. *(Pause.)* I also have been thinking
a lot about the things we talked about last time.

P 3: Would you like to tell me about some of the
things you have been thinking about?

R 3: Well, it's sort of strange. One day I feel real good
and think that I will be able to stay out of trouble
from now on, but then the next day I wouldn't
be sure. I'd find myself thinking up things to do
and wondering if I could get away with them.

P 4: At times you feel the future is going to be all
right, but at other times you're not so sure.
*(His response "tacks down" the ambivalence ex-
pressed in R 3.)*

R 4: Yeah, but I just can't figure out why I think
about ways of breaking into places and things
like that. I guess it's good that I'm in here and all
I can do is think about doing such things.

P 5: You're not sure if you could control these im-
pulses if you were on the outside.
(He zeros in on the problem.)

R 5: No, I'm not sure that I could. That's just how it
was before; I'd get the idea to do some crazy

thing and if I thought I had a 50-50 chance of getting away with it, I'd try it.

P 6: You did some of these things just to see if you could get away with them.

(This is an interpretation by the pastor rather than by the counselee.)

R 6: Yeah. *(He was silent for a long time, then he began talking again, speaking very softly.)* I guess that's not the only reason, and that's just what bothers me. I just can't understand why I do these things. Sometimes it was almost like a dream. I'd wake up in the morning and think I dreamed that I had done something wrong. Then I'd find some money in my jacket, or some things in my car, and then I'd know it wasn't a dream.

(At first he passively agrees to the pastor's interpretation. But as the pastor wisely waits out the pause, the counselee is able to express his misgivings over the interpretation. He has the characteristic human need to "tell it like it is." The point he wants to make is that his motivation is a mystery, and this frightens him.)

P 7: How did you feel when you discovered that you had actually done these things?

R 7: It sort of bothered me. I'd worry about getting caught.

(A candid answer.)

P 8: You were afraid that someone would find out about it.

R 8: I guess I was; but not just because I was afraid of what would happen to me. I was afraid that my folks would find out; and I just don't want to hurt them again. *(At this point the inmate was nervously fiddling with his hands, and his eyes were beginning to water a little.)* I've already done so much to hurt them, I couldn't stand to hurt them again. I've caused them so much trouble, and they keep trying to help me. When I'd get into trouble, they'd get real strict for a while and tell me that they knew I'd grow up and start behaving myself. Then I'd do better for a while, but before long I'd be in trouble again.

P 9: Do you feel your parents were too strict with you?

R 9: No, that's just it. They usually weren't very strict at all—just when I would get in trouble. I don't blame them though. But I actually think they should have treated me rougher. Even then I thought that, but yet I resented their punishment; it made me mad.

(Here is the predicament of parenthood. The very discipline he knows he needs from his parents he also resents receiving. The inconsistency of the counselee's parents at this point may be a contributing factor to his problem in relating to them, and perhaps also to society as a whole.)

P10: You felt they should punish you, yet when they did, you resented it.

(He again tacks down the ambivalent attitude.)

R10: Yes, I almost felt like going out and doing something real terrible; I just can't seem to do what's right. If they were strict, I couldn't live up to it, but when they were lenient I didn't even keep out of trouble either. I—I just can't seem to do what's right, no matter what.

P11: You just can't seem to do what they expect of you.

(He accepts the counselee's interpretation of his impotency.)

R11: No, I've never been able to; all I've ever done is cause trouble for them and hurt them. It isn't right. They've done so much for me, and I don't deserve it. Sometimes I thought they'd be better off if I'd go away somewhere, but that would hurt, I know it would. Once when I was down in K—— and I got in trouble, I even thought of drowning myself in the river. The only thing that stopped me was I realized that would also hurt them. I guess it would have been better if I never had them as parents, but then I'd probably be in deeper trouble, like killing someone or something; but at least I wouldn't have hurt them.

P12: There just doesn't seem to be an answer to your problem.

(He accepts the counselee's despair—the most difficult of all emotional attitudes with which to empathize.)

R12: No, there doesn't. I just can't seem to keep out of trouble, but mom and dad keep trying to keep me out of trouble.

P13: They try harder than you, it seems. You do resist them, don't you?

R13: Yeah—and afterward I feel guilty.

P14: But what do you feel before—when you're resisting them?

R14: I guess I'm mad.

P15: At them?

R15: Yeah—they piss me off—nag me to go to church —to come home early at night. Yet I know they mean it well.

P16: You believe they care about you—love you.

R16: I really do—which makes me feel all the worse for the way I act.

P17: Do you find it hard to forgive yourself?

R17: In a way, but I just don't deserve all that my folks have done for me. They sure must love me a lot, but look what I've done. I don't deserve it; I'm no good. I don't deserve to have anyone do anything for me. *(At this point the inmate nervously was trying to get a cigarette out of a package. As he was doing this, he kept talking along the line of the foregoing subject. He attempted to light the cigarette, but it didn't light. He didn't seem to notice this because he kept trying to flick off ashes in the ashtray. His eyes were now red, but he wasn't outwardly crying. The counselee's guilt at the moment is overshadowing his hostility toward his parents. Since it is guilt that is uppermost in his consciousness, the counselor responds to it.)*

P18: You just can't see anything good in yourself at all. *(He "descends into hell" with him—a necessary prerequisite to any attempt to assist him with a solution.)*

R18: No, I can't. Look at all the trouble I've caused.

P19: Bob, I realize that you have been rebelling against your parents' religion, but do you know that God loves you and will accept you as you are? *(In my opinion, a natural opening for a pastor to raise this question.)*

R19: Oh, yes, I've been taught that. I've always thought that God would forgive a person if he asked God to forgive him on his deathbed, but then I have often even told myself that I could do this myself, that I could do this or that just once more and he'd forgive me. *(An existential expression of Bonhoeffer's concept of cheap grace.)*

P20: Well, Bob, we can't test God's love that way, but God will accept us as we are. No matter what we have done or what we are, he will forgive us if we confess our sins to him. God will do this because he loves us; and he loves each one of us so much that he allowed his own Son Jesus Christ to be crucified for our sins. When we accept and experience God's love, then we will change our ways out of love and gratitude for what he has done for us. Do you understand what I mean, Bob? *(The pastor obviously did not receive the response to his injection of God-talk that he anticipated.*

In a sense the counselee rejected it. So the pastor is thrown on the defensive and begins to pound home his point.)

R20: I think so, but so many people think that I'm no good. When I was home before it seemed at first that everyone was trying to accept me and forget about what I had done, but then the folks of the fellows I got in trouble with didn't want me around their places anymore.

(A painful experience of rejection.)

P21: Well, you see, Bob, most people aren't able to accept other people as they are, because they usually love people on the basis of what they are going to get in return. In other words, if someone goes against them, then they withdraw their love and acceptance. You see, they really don't know what love is. God's love is just the opposite: he loves us in spite of our sins and the wrong things we have done. His love is unconditional. *(The inmate seemed much calmer at this point, and smiled.)* Does this make sense to you, Bob?

(Since he is caught up in the momentum of his own defensiveness, he is too preoccupied to empathize and compulsively presses on, relying on many words and his systematic theology to counteract the counselee's resistance.)

R21: I—I think so.

(An eloquent contrast to Bob's previous involvement. He feels the coercion to conform.)

P22: Do you feel that I have accepted you, Bob, even though you have told me all that you have done? *(Fortunately he did not continue, but rather changed the focus from God to himself.)*

R22: Yeah, I think so. I've even wondered about that. I know you don't have to come out here to see me; I guess you must feel I can be helped, or you wouldn't take the time to talk to me. And I do feel a lot better now that I have talked to you about all of these things. I've never been able to even talk to anyone about it before. I know now that even if I won't be able to see you again, at least I won't be afraid to talk to someone about these things.

(Relieved, Bob becomes involved again. The pressure associated with God-talk is gone.)

P23: It is more out in the open now.

(The pastor is a counselor again, relaxed and responding.)

R23: Yes, that's about right; I'm not so afraid that people will find out now. It feels so easy to talk about it. You know, when I was down to see that doctor before I came here, the first thing he told me was that what I would say would only be between me and him and wouldn't leave the office. Then on the way home I found out that while I was filling out some test, he was out in the other room talking to my folks, and they knew everything that I told him. After that I just didn't think I could tell anyone about these things, like torturing the animals and everything else.

P24: Are you afraid that I might do the same?

R24: No, I'm not. It seems kind of funny; it—it just doesn't seem to bother me that way now.

P25: I'm sorry, Bob, but I guess we will have to close for now. I think you would find what we have talked about more meaningful if tonight when you are back in your cell, you'd read over 1 John 1:9 and John 3:16.

(He suddenly remembers his unfinished business and tries desperately to wrap things up. Naively he believes the counselee will remember such references, even carry out the assignment.)

R25: I'll do that. Will I be able to see you again next week?

> *(The counselor succeeds in spite of his problems*
> *over God-talk. The inmate is more interested in*
> *seeing* him *than in the assignment. The relation-*
> *ship is a positive influence in itself.)*

P26: I won't be here for the next two weeks, Bob, but
I will see you that following week if you would
like that.

R26: Yes, I'd like that. I really appreciate being able to
talk to you.

It was the counselee's negative reaction to the pastor's verbalization of the gospel (R19) that marked the change in the
direction of the session. The pastor failed to respond, because
it seemed to be a repudiation of what religiously he was trying
to offer. Suppose that instead of reacting defensively to R19, he
could have been secure enough with God-talk to have responded something like the following:

> P20: In other words it hasn't been much incentive to
> you to do better.

This would have changed the direction of the conversation
from defending his offering to taking a serious look at Bob's
resistance. Also it would have allowed P19 to be an honest
question.

If the inmate's recollection of painful rejection in R20 were
a challenge to the counselor to empathize rather than to debate,
he may have responded with an awareness of Bob's feelings.

> P21: That must have hurt!

This would have encouraged Bob to go further into his experiences of rejection that had moved him to withdraw into himself (R22, R23), so that the Good News of God's acceptance
was met only with calculated exploitation (R19).

These two responding alternates to the pastor's reactions show how inevitable is his directive role in the counseling process. There is no such thing as nondirective counseling; there are only alternative ways of directing.

The difference in the number of words used by the pastor is also interesting. When he is in a responding role (P1 through P18) his verbalizing is only one-fourth that of the counselee. However, after Bob's resistance to God-talk, the situation is completely reversed. Now it is the pastor whose words quadruple those of the counselee (P20 though R21). When God-talk is no longer involved (P22 through R24), the proportions return to what they were before.

It would seem, then, that when the pastor met resistance to his introduction of God-talk, he felt compelled to convince the counselee. In Pauline analogues, he tried to *sow, water,* and *reap* all in one operation. His alternative as a counselor is to be content to sow—to work under the Holy Spirit. We need to trust that the Holy Spirit can work after the pastoral counseling event as well as during it, and through subsequent people and experiences as well as through us and our counseling. In fact, other experiences may be necessary for the counselee before he can fully appropriate the value of his counseling experience. To trust in the Holy Spirit's guidance means to be able to tolerate the tension of resistance and the lack of consensus in matters close to our professional identity. Even in his resistance to God-talk, we need to hear the counselee. Pressing hard via the filibuster route to solicit a consensus, the pastor reduced Bob to a head-nodding parishioner. The head-nodding is the alternative to dialogue, the sign that the session has degenerated into a monologue, the evidence that the counselee is really no longer involved. Our desire as counselors to solicit a consensus from the counselee may stem from our need for reassurance that we are right. Trusting in the Holy Spirit's guidance allows us the vulnerability of being wrong.

The Tension of Confrontation

When God-talk is introduced by the counselee and the pastor responds, the movement is usually smoother than when the pastor introduces it. When I sense the counselee is open to the question, I may ask, "Have you been able to pray about this?" While this is an assertive approach, it is in line with the pastoral counselor's vocational identity. It is our way of opening the dialogue to the realm of the spirit—of the divine-human encounter. The dialogical principle also allows for the legitimacy of the question. In a dialogue both counselee and counselor are free to provide input to the direction of the session. The major qualification concerning both our response to the counselee's introduction of God-talk and our own assertive interjection of it is that we do so *dialogically*. Can we sense when our insertion is "with the flow" of the dialogue—when the counselee is open to the question? Can we also give the counselee the freedom to respond, and can we accept the response, even when it is a negative reaction? If we develop these abilities, we are "in" for exciting "trips" into depths of being usually blocked off from those who are "uptight" over this route, either because of their defensiveness toward religion or because of their skepticism regarding its value.

The following counseling verbatim is an illustration of these depths and of the dialogical approach in God-talk that led both counselor and counselee to them. The counselee is a successful middle-aged businessman who had just informed his wife that he wanted a divorce. He accepted his pastor's invitation to talk it over. The excerpt is from the first visit.

> MAN: No matter who gets hurt—my wife, sons—I must do what I have to do.
> PASTOR: And what is it you have to do?
> M: To fulfill my life. If I don't do it now, I never will.
> P: And this means leaving your wife?
> M: I don't see any other way. She's been a good wife in

many ways—an excellent mother to our sons—but I've been lonely in the marriage. I'm sort of mystical, and she's very practical. I've told her this.

P: I understand from her that she realizes this and is desirous to make changes.

M: It's too late. She didn't hear me all those years.

P: You have other plans now?

M: What do you mean?

P: Well, this is the sort of thing you would have loved to have heard previously. Now you hear it and you are not happy about it.

M: I see what you mean. Yes, there are some things I'd like to investigate.

P: And you can't do them being married to your wife.

M: No. I wouldn't feel right about it. There's a woman in the office. We get along well. It's just possible we could strike up something. I'd like to be free to give it a try.

P: Your interests are really toward this other possibility, so there's not much interest left in your marriage.

M: You put it crassly, but I guess that's right.

P: You mentioned that you want to feel right about it.

M: Yes. I don't believe in hanky-pankying around.

P: In a sense you've already done this in your plans and interests.

M: Yes. I suppose that's why I want a divorce—because I want to investigate the possibility. I want to be free to do this.

P: You have mentioned how you feel morally. How about religiously?

M: Hmm. *(Pause)* My religion is mostly my morality, I'm afraid. I believe in right and wrong. I believe in the church. As you know, I've chairmanned a few committees over the years.

P: You said you believe in the church. Do you believe in God?

M: Yes—but I'm not really religious in that sense.

Never have been. I always get queasy when I hear talk about prayer at church. I'm more comfortable talking about ethics or community service in church life.

P: You don't pray, then.

M: No—not really. I've read prayers at church on occasion—and bow my head when others have prayed, but— *(pause)*.

P: Nothing goes on *inside* you.

M: No.

P: Pretty empty there—lonely.

M: Yes. I don't know why.

P: God is more of an idea to think about for you than a person to know and to pray to.

M: Right. The nearest I get—something my wife has not been able to share with me—is a feeling of something—when I see a beautiful sunset—or stars on a dark night—or the dawn. I just want to be quiet—and look.

(The pastor had the choice either to continue in this inward look or to focus on the lack of companionship alluded to with the wife. He chose the former, not wishing to encourage a distraction at this point, knowing that he could pick up the marital allusion later.)

P: Would you like to be able to talk to God—or to listen to him?

M: I don't know. That seems so foreign to me.

P: Nobody has really become that close to you, have they—close enough to share with from your inside?

M: I guess I've been a loner there. I'm not sure I could ever change.

P: You're used to it—and yet you do want to change. You said you wanted to experience fulfillment. Wouldn't this be part of fulfillment?

M: I'm blocking now. My mind's not focusing.

P: What about your feelings? What are you feeling now?

M: Uncomfortable.

P: Do you want to stop what we are doing?

M: I'm not sure. Maybe I'm seeing something I really need to see.

What the man was beginning to see was that while he had many involvements with people, these involvements centered in discussions and activities external to his own inner world. Inwardly, as he acknowledged, he had been a "loner." He opened himself within neither to his wife nor to God. Obviously something *was* lacking in his life—something obstructing his fulfillment—and in midlife he had become painfully aware of it. As was subsequently revealed, the "rough" beginnings of his life predisposed him to hide behind an aggressive exterior. Although those early days were long over, the now dated habit of hiding continued and was blocking his development. Yet this behavior had not been challenged previously because his aggressive exterior had seemed to serve him well in the business world.

The man was getting an "insight" into himself. Some counselors such as Reality Therapist William Glasser are opposed to what they call "insight therapy." Obviously if one concentrates only on his past in the search for self-understanding, he may be distracted from responsibilities that can be assumed in the "here and now." On the other hand the "here and now" may have much to do with the "there and then." If so, understanding the input from the past into the present could be helpful in coping intelligently with the present. Insight is not the equivalent of resolving or overcoming, but it can be a step, and often a necessary step, to resolving and overcoming. It provides the needed light on the problem when otherwise we may grope in darkness. Yet one needs to act on the insight. Otherwise it may become simply another escape from responsibility, as one continually seeks for more understanding rather than acting on the understanding one has.

When I was a child, I had a cereal bowl that had the words "Find the Bottom" printed on the upper inside portion. On the bottom of the bowl was a picture of Peter Rabbit—and seeing it come into view was the incentive to finishing one's cereal. There are counselees who play the game, "Find the Bottom." "I'm just not sure," said one of these, "whether we have really gotten to the bottom of things. It doesn't seem to me that we have." He said this in response to a series of insights, all of which could have been liberating influences for action, but they were not. Because such persons are reluctant to take the responsible action that is needed to cope with their problems, the game of "finding the bottom" can be an endless diversion.

In the session with M it was the pastor's interjection of God-talk and dialogical follow-up that led to the intrapersonal dimension of M's life which he had by long years of habit sealed off—initially for his own survival—from others. As was evident from the dialogue, insight is more than an intellectual perception. As Wise puts it in *Pastoral Counseling,* "Insight is an emotional grasp of elements which comprise the personality." What M does with his insight into himself is of course not predisposed by the insight itself. One of the purposes of counseling is to assist one to see what is involved in one's difficulties so that one can act more intelligently and realistically in these difficulties.

Summary

God-talk is a counseling resource stemming directly from the context of the specific faith of pastoral counseling. It is an asset to the counseling process since its symbols pertain to the basic issues of human life. The criterion for its use depends upon the context of the counseling session—what is going on in the relationship that may or may not reveal an openness to this resource. Pastors need also to take stock of their own predispositions regarding God-talk. Is one attempting to "prove" something in using or not using it? Only when this is faced and dealt with is one free to decide on the basis of the context whether or not to use God-talk. When the counselee initiates God-talk into the relationship, the counselor, as an expression of this freedom, needs to be sensitive to the reason for this initiation. Drawing persons out on what the God-talk means to them is one way of ascertaining this. Pastors cannot be sure that what the God-talk symbols mean to them are also what they mean to the counselee. Seeking clarification on the use of the symbols also helps the person to clarify his or her own theological insights. Our own clarity of belief increases as we attempt to articulate this belief to another.

The criteria for the pastor's interjection of God-talk into the counseling session would depend on his or her sensitivity to the other's openness for it—or at least an openness for an inquiry into its significance in the person's life. Should the pastor misjudge this openness—for all such sensitivity involves the risk of error—the dialogue on the resistance can be a revealing experience for both counselor and counselee, providing the pastor does not become defensive over the resistance. The significant dialogue that follows may lead to a more intelligent approach to the disturbance that brought the person into counseling. The dialogical medium within which a counseling use of God-talk is conducted is itself a protection against abuses of God-talk and a disposition for its effectiveness.

6

Scripture
and
Meditation

A familiar traditional pastoral resource, the Bible is the written basis for the specific faith of pastoral care and counseling. Its value as a resource for pastoral care and counseling derives from the belief that the Bible is the Word of God, although how this is understood may vary. In this capacity it is much used and also much abused. As the Word of God the Bible is not simply a book with inspiring thoughts and stories, but a book through which the Spirit of God speaks.

The Bible as the Word

While the Word of God has other forms than the Bible, none of these is separated from it. As the "Word made flesh" who "dwelt among us" Christ himself is the living Word—the revelation of God in a human life. His gospel is also referred to as the Word. The preaching of the gospel, for example, is also called the proclamation of the Word. Yet what we know about Christ and his gospel is all related to what is in the Bible. Preaching, for example, is frequently based upon a scriptural text.

As the Word of God through which God reveals himself to his people, the Bible is a *means,* not an *end.* As such it is a *means of grace*. In its misuse the Bible is converted into an ultimate authority—an end in itself. Converting a means into an end is basically what is meant by idolatry, and there are no means more susceptible to this distortion than religious symbols. When this happens to the Bible, the flexibility of the Holy Spirit is replaced by the rigidity of the Holy Book. The Bible's value to pastoral care depends on its mediatorial function: it is a means by which the Spirit bears "witness with our spirits that we are the children of God" (Rom. 8:16), that it is "profitable for teaching, for reproof, for correction, and for training in righteousness" (2 Tim. 3:16).

One of the divisive issues among Christians is the critical study of the Bible. Although this is primarily the responsibility of the biblical scholars, such study is related also to pastoral care. The purpose of critical study is to assist the reader in perceiving the historical and social context in which the biblical documents were written. Since the first Christian community existed without the New Testament as we know it, another purpose for critical study is to determine the relationship of this community to the writing, editing, and collecting of this canon. If the purpose of critical study is to understand the meaning of the various biblical teachings to its immediate community context, the ultimate purpose is to assist in ascertaining its meaning for our time and context.

As a means of grace and not an end in itself, the Bible can and should be subjected to critical study. Though inspired by God, it is also written by human writers and compiled by human editors. These writers and editors, in addition to their devotion and openness to God's Spirit, were also influenced by the time and culture in which they lived. It is helpful in ascertaining the transcultural nature of the Word of God to perceive the cultural clothing into which it was of necessity first presented.

Yet critical study—like all scientific pursuits—has its limits, which unfortunately have not always been observed. Because the Scripture is a means of grace, it has meaning that critical study alone cannot fathom. Such study needs to be balanced by a devotional use of the Scripture in which the focus is not primarily the objective discipline of the scientific mind, but the subjective discipline of listening to the Word. As a means of grace the Bible is also a medium for our dialogue with the Spirit of God. This dialogue also provides us with knowledge of the Bible. Like the scientific approach it too has its limits, which also unfortunately have not always been observed. Each approach needs the other for its own balance.

The Spirit speaks through the Word in the milieu of the church. The Bible was not only produced by the church, but also given to the church. It is a means of grace for the church's ministry. While the church is an institution in society like other institutions, it is also more than an institution: it is the "body of Christ," the community of faith, the tangible presence of God's people. Pastoral care and counseling are specific expressions of the ministry of this community. The pastoral counselor has a resource in the Bible that is organically related to his or her specific form of ministry. Ordained pastors are prepared in varying degrees by their theological education in the knowledge of the Bible and in the ministry of pastoral care and counseling. They are, therefore, in a position to assist their counselees to hear the Word of God in their particular needs.

I recall in my own theological education reading the books of John Sutherland Bonnell, who in those days taught pastoral care and counseling at Princeton Theological Seminary. I particularly remember Bonnell's approach to the Scripture. A specific example that stayed with me concerned a hospital patient who was in great anxiety about her impending surgery. Bonnell listened empathetically to her fears and then offered her a word from Scripture to take with her to her surgery. It was Psalm 34:4: "I sought the Lord, and he answered me, and delivered me from all my fears." He used the verse in his prayer with her and then copied it for her so that she could have it continually with her. Actually he was teaching her to meditate on the Word, although he could not have so described it at that time. I used Bonnell's approach early in my ministry under similar circumstances.

Pastoral Care of Sufferers

As Bonnell's approach indicates, the Bible is used frequently in the pastoral care of the sick. As indicated previously, the differentiation between pastoral care and pastoral counseling is difficult to delineate in crisis ministry. The pastor may enter into a crisis ministry with pastoral care and, because of the effect of the crisis on the person, shift to pastoral counseling. The biblical sufferer, Job, for example, experienced many reverses in his crisis: he lost his children, his wealth, his social status, and his health. For these he needed the support of pastoral care through his friends. But these losses led to a spiritual crisis. He felt betrayed by God. How else could he interpret what had happened? For his despair, rage, and spiritual turmoil he needed also pastoral counseling.

In the supportive ministry to those afflicted by the adversities of life, the Scripture may serve an important purpose. For instance, the Jobian protest, "Why?" "Why me?" is a frequent reaction in these adversities. As a biblical sufferer, Job himself provides a ready identification for the afflicted. One sufferer to whom I ministered, for example, tried to accept her terminal illness "like a Christian." She had been conditioned to speak only the words of pious acceptance in her tribulations. By denying any resentment, she believed she was being obedient to God. I talked with her about Job and read to her some of Job's emotional outpourings, in the hope that it would help her to accept her own feelings. The authority of the Bible, in the context of my authority as its symbol bearer, gave her the permission she needed to acknowledge that she too had a conflict. "I keep wondering," she said, "if I'm being punished for something—something that I have done—or perhaps have *not* done? Like Job, I guess I wish God would tell me what it is that he has against me!"

In his ordeal of crucifixion Jesus himself identified with a biblical character. The writer of Psalm 22 provided him with the words he needed to express how he felt. "My God, my God, why hast thou forsaken me?" I had occasion to use these words in a recent visit to a woman who had experienced one blow after another. When I inquired whether her faith had been helpful to her, she replied, "I guess I'm not much of a Christian."

"What makes you think that?" I asked.

"Some friends were here," she said. "They told me that I should be praising the Lord for all my troubles, and really I don't feel that way."

I asked her if she remembered how Jesus felt when he suffered. When she seemed uncertain in her recall I reminded her. "He said, 'My God, my God, why hast thou forsaken me?'"

After a moment of silence I asked her if these words expressed the way she felt at times. "They surely do," she said.

"You can't be too bad of a Christian if you feel like Jesus," I said.

"It's not the same," she said. "After all, he was God. He knew how things were going to turn out—and I don't." Her reaction led us to a dialogue in God-talk about the Incarnation.

"You're right," I said. "If he were God and only God, he wouldn't have really been one of us. But what about his humanity—that he was also like us in every way?"

"I don't understand that," she said.

"I don't say I understand it either," I said. "But something St. Paul said helps me, and maybe it will help you. He said Christ 'emptied' himself in order to be like us. Perhaps, then, he emptied himself even of this knowledge about how things were going to turn out—so that he really didn't know at that moment—and then he felt just like you."

God's empathy with human suffering is a symbol of his caring. We need this symbol in order to trust him. As a hospital chaplain I have been impressed by the way Roman Catholic patients identify with Christ in their sufferings by their reflection on the stations of the cross.

Although in his pastoral care of the sick the pastor may pray with the patient for healing, healing may not come. Beside being disappointed, or bitter, the patient may wonder whether his continuing illness is due to his lack of faith. Some of his religious visitors may reenforce him in this impression. In blaming himself, he may be shifting his resentment over his illness to himself—a safer target than either the pastor or God.

While the pastor needs to take seriously the patient's feelings of disappointment and anger, he or she needs also to deal with the relationship between faith and healing. Not everybody who has faith is healed of illness—not even in the Bible. Paul, who was instrumental in healing others, was not healed of his own "thorn in the flesh," even though he prayed repeatedly for healing. It might help the disappointed patient to know of another disappointed patient with whom he or she can identify, particularly since Paul was able to move beyond his disappointment. Although the thorn in the flesh remained, ultimately he learned to live positively with it. "My grace is sufficient for you, for my power is made perfect in weakness" (2 Cor. 12:9). Healing may come in ways other than we anticipate.

In times of affliction when people are troubled by what to them is God's absence, the Word of the Scripture may become the symbol of his presence. The pastor's judicious use of Scripture in pastoral care may stimulate encouragement and hope in the midst of circumstances that otherwise could leave one discouraged and hopeless.

In their afflictions some people have much difficulty in managing their feelings. They may worry, for example, about whether they will ever become well, and the anxiety may overwhelm them. Sharing these feelings with the pastor helps to release the pressure. Anxiety, however, feeds on attention. After expressing it, one needs to let go of it—in religious language, to surrender it to God. Because of habit patterns this may be difficult. Here again, the Scripture may be helpful. Jesus' words, "Do not be afraid, only believe," can be personalized by the pastor to the anxious sufferer. Paul's exhortation, "Let the peace of God rule in your hearts," indicates that we tend to resist God's peace. Anxiety's hold on us is also our hold on it. The exhortation from God through his Word to "let peace rule," is an encouragement to the sufferer to trust.

We can be overwhelmed also by feelings of discouragement and futility. We may experience more reverses than we seemingly can tolerate, and we need help to keep from slipping into the "slough of despond." The pastor may augment his care of such persons by assisting them to hear Christ's words: "Come unto me you who are heavy laden . . . and I will give you rest." The Psalms are also helpful as they express the gamut of human feelings. As devotional hymns they speak to the heart: their identification with despondency forms a bridge to hope. "Out of the depths have I cried unto thee, O Lord." "Why art thou cast down O my soul . . . Hope thou in God, for I shall yet praise him."

Some sufferers are overcome by guilt. Feeling under judgment, they make themselves miserable by their self-loathing, and they need pastoral assistance or permission to cease their self-punishing ways. Some are weary of this never-ending abuse. As one expressed it to me, "I'm fed up with hating myself!" He wanted to be free from this bondage. The words of Jesus spoken to another sinner gave him a start. "Neither do I condemn you." Also the Old Testament assurance, "As far as the east is from the west, so far has he removed our transgressions from us" (Ps. 103:12).

There are times when little can be done to change a bad situation. The challenge is not to make it worse. One is tempted under the stress to "settle" the matter by actions which may terminate any remaining hope for change. This is often the case, for instance, in marriage and family crises when what little hope there is for reconciliation depends on keeping open the doors. Instead one may overreact in panic or anger and destroy any remaining possibilities. The pastor's counseling is an influence against such overreacting. It can be reenforced by devotional practices which help those who are distraught to "wait on the Lord."

In other stress situations a person may need encouragement to act. Because one fails to act—often because of fear—the situation may go from bad to worse. Although people in these straits may know what they should do, they may be immobilized by fear or by lack of confidence. The pastoral relationship itself can strengthen their confidence to act. Within this relationship reflecting on Scripture, like the parable of the pearl of great price, may further assist these people to take the risks that are necessary to achieve their desires. The importance in their taking the initiative is stressed by the words, "Ask, and it will be given you; seek, and you will find; knock, and it will be opened to you" (Matt. 7:7).

Beneficial Rather Than Detrimental Use of Scripture

Unfortunately, the Scripture has been used by the church for purposes other than healing. Pastors have used it badly as well as wisely. In tense moments it is a temptation to resort to an authority such as the Bible to bring a quick answer. This is often at the expense of fully investigating the problem or of facing reality. Since few of us enjoy an emotionally charged atmosphere, pastor and counselee may subconsciously collaborate to avoid any painful encounters. They try to bring in the light without entering into the darkness. Pastors, like others, are fearful of getting into more than they think they can handle. In discussing his verbatim of a pastoral visit, I asked a pastor if he was aware of his consistent avoidance of the counselee's negative feelings. "I was aware," he said, "but I was afraid to draw her out—because I wasn't sure I could cope with what might have come out." While it is wise to recognize our limits, it is also befitting our vocation to grow in our competency.

We may also avoid a direct response to the negative for fear of stirring up our own inner "hornets' nest." We all have our vulnerable areas, and it is wise to recognize them so that we do not project them into our counseling relationships. Yet if we are aware of these problems, we should get the help we need to come to terms with them.

Rather than using the Bible to evade the facing of reality, the pastor may use it to facilitate such facing. In order to attain the genuinely positive, one needs to enter into the genuinely negative. To do this, however, we need a vision of "light at the end of the tunnel." Without it, the darkness could overwhelm us. To evade the negative as long as possible would then make sense. But if there is light ahead, such evasion is ultimately self-destructive.

Our natural tendency is to run from any thoughts or feelings that make us uncomfortable. The pastor's way of running is quickly to reassure the counselee at the mere mention of the negative. I have misused the Bible at times to reenforce this reassurance when I lacked the courage to draw the person out on the negative. Similar to the previously mentioned pastor, I was probably not sure I could or even wanted to deal with such feelings if they did come out. When we use the Bible to stifle the expression of the negative, we are treating the symptoms at the expense of the source in a most superficial manner. I have learned the hard way to use the Bible in these instances to provide the support for the counselee to look *into* the negative.

In our culture one of the most difficult of these negatives to face is hostility. Usually other negatives such as anxiety or guilt will be shared more easily. Consequently, the pastoral counselor needs to listen not only to what is being expressed, but also for what is not being expressed. Usually we share the feelings that are least threatening to us—that we deem to be most acceptable. We may not even be aware of the more threatening feelings within us until we express the less threatening, and it may come as a jolt when we recognize hatred and vindictiveness within our own being. As trust grows, the counselee may hint at these more difficult areas, and the sensitive pastor will respond to these hints.

Probably the most feared of the dark passions is despair. In my observation it is the mental state that pastors find most difficult to accept and to identify with. This is because despair contains both desperation and terror. Should vestiges of it be lurking within our own psyche, feeling with another's despair could resurrect our own. The agony of hopelessness is more than many of us can tolerate. Yet Jesus' cry of abandonment on the cross—together with other similar laments in the Bible —shows the relevancy of the gospel to this most dreaded of moods.

As a church we have been able to cope best with the negativity of guilt. Our cultic rites have focused on the liturgical forms for confession and absolution. Yet because the rite for private confession is so rarely used in our day, pastors may even find the pain in confession too discomforting to endure. Instead they may prematurely attempt to relieve the pain, rushing in with the reassurance of forgiveness before the confession has run its course. Confession includes contrition. People need to face the full scope of the judgment that they are experiencing. The painful sharing of the guilt opens the person to receive the gift of forgiveness. If this sharing is interrupted by a premature offering of the gift, the opening process is impeded. Also we pastors may not realize all that is included in our reassurance. Since the confessee has not had the opportunity to share the whole story, the absolution he or she receives may remain too abstract to be healing. Since the full sharing of the negative is itself a part of the healing process, we need to hold back on our reassurance until we have dealt adequately with the confession.

Prophetic Use of Scripture in Counseling

The use of Scripture in pastoral counseling is not just for comfort and strength but also for direction and guidance. In the record of his temptation in the wilderness Jesus used his knowledge of the Old Testament to affirm his identity in each of his ordeals: in the temptation to relieve his hunger by turning stones into bread: "Man shall not live by bread alone, but by every word that proceeds from the mouth of God"; in the temptation to attract followers by jumping from the top of the temple: "You shall not tempt the Lord your God"; in the temptation to worship the devil to secure the kingdoms of the world: "You shall worship the Lord your God and him only shall you serve" (Matt. 4:1-10). In each instance Jesus made a choice regarding his behavior and aspirations. He used the Scripture for guidance and for support in the shaping of his ministry. So also God's people need to reflect upon their decisions and behavior in the light of their religious tradition as it is recorded in the Bible.

This use of the Bible can be designated as a *prophetic* use, in differentiation to the *priestly* use which we have been describing. The prophetic use—patterned after the socially conscious biblical prophets—pertains to the *vocation* of God's people. While a priestly use focuses on personal problems and ills, the prophetic use focuses on one's calling to serve God. As defined by Paul, the vocational challenge is our response to the Good News: "You are not your own; you were bought with a price. So glorify God in your body" (1 Cor. 6:19-20). The Petrine literature stresses the corporate nature of this vocation: "But you are a chosen race, a royal priesthood, a holy nation, God's own people, that you may declare the wonderful deeds of him who called you out of darkness into his marvelous light" (1 Pet. 2:9). We are not only receivers, but also givers.

Pastors may often counsel with people who are not aware of a sense of vocation or who may not even be Christians. A basic principle of all counseling is that the counselor begins where the counselee is. Yet pastors bring with them—even to those not associated with the Christian faith—their own perception of human life. There is a vision—a calling—that gives life its meaning and purpose. The basic position of logotherapy, for example, is that one needs such a sense of meaning in order to live humanly or perhaps even to survive. Logotherapy is *logos-therapy,* and *logos* is the New Testament word for the *Word.* Similarly in the book of Acts, the gospel is described as the Way. Those who receive are also called to a specific way of living.

The prophetic dimension to pastoral counseling is based on the theological position that one is not one's own. We do not live for ourselves—even for our own happiness—but for the One who has redeemed us with his "costly grace." Because of our preoccupation with the priestly ministry of healing, we may neglect the prophetic ministry of challenging those who receive also to give. Unfortunately when we do become prophetic in our counseling, we may do it badly. It is tempting to resort to one's responsibility before God as a club to coerce a resistant counselee into line. The nature of prophetic religion makes it susceptible to legalistic distortion. When rules and roles become rigid, they are usually heavily conditioned by cultural values. Outer performance then becomes more important than inner quality.

Pastors may encounter a legalistic understanding of Christian vocation in their counseling—particularly in marriage and family counseling. Parents locked in conflict with their older children who are rebelling against the parents' religious and moral standards, for example, may justify their rejection of them on the basis of God's judgment of sin. The pastor, however, can utilize their biblical orientation to help them to break through their rigidity. After listening not only to their anger, but also to their hurt and humiliation, he or she can dialogue with them on related Scriptures. The pastor can, for instance, renew their acquaintance with a biblical family in which there was trouble between a caring parent and an erring child. The picture of God as the father of the prodigal son may give them a different insight into their options. When they see that even good parents can have trouble with their children, and that the conforming elder brother may not be the ideal, they may be less hard on themselves as parental failures. When they see that even God has to wait for his prodigal son to return, they may not feel so frustrated by their own powerlessness. The model of the hurt but forgiving father may begin to have its effect.

Another role rigidity encountered today is over the so-called male headship of a family. Pearl, for example, was locked in conflict over this with her husband. She believed that her marriage was stifling her own identity. Pete, however, resisted any change by defending his dominating ways on the basis of his role as the head of his wife. He was living the model of the male role with which he grew up. His mother never complained; so why then should Pearl be dissatisfied? Since his parents justified the way they did things by the Bible, Pete was doing the same. That there were other ways than domination of defining male headship had not seemed to occur to him.

People who justify their insensitivity to the needs of others by their supposed fidelity to biblical models are not going to change simply by hearing a different approach to these models. They may even become defensive as a result. Yet a compassionate pastor may be able to penetrate such rigid defense systems by engaging in a dialogue on the biblical context of the word *head*, as it refers to Christ as the model. His headship is described as "one who serves," and when applied to marriage, as loving one's wife as oneself (Luke 22:27; Eph. 5:33). Pearl's behavior is important also in effecting this change. Pete too has needs that she can help to meet. As one is pleased, one tends to please.

A hermeneutical case can be made that *headship* is a first-century symbol, and that it is more possible in our day to search for symbols in line with the parallel biblical understanding of the equality of male and female in Christ. The point at issue in this instance, however, is in relating to the counselee where he is. The epistle writer's own description of headship eliminated it as a defense for Pete's need to dominate Pearl. Pete could receive this understanding because it was presented as the biblical writer's own interpretation. Without this defense Pete was more vulnerable—and in this instance more open because of the warm and respectful approach of the pastor— to a critical evaluation of his behavior.

The pastor can be helpful, however, in the stresses of marriage and family that stem from the changing roles of men and women in our society. "There is neither male nor female; for you are all one in Christ Jesus" (Gal. 3:28). How does this principle apply to life in the family in our day? Even as the New Testament writers applied the gospel to the cultural forms for the family of the first century, we have this same obligation to do so in our own generation. If this process is carried out in a spirit of dialogue, defensive persons feel less threatened and may even catch a glimpse of a more challenging vocation in their family relations.

Another familiar marital stress concerns the spouse who permits parents to dominate the marriage because of a dated perception of what it means to honor them. Although the partner resents the interference, the spouse protests that he or she cannot bear to see the parents hurt. "They don't mean to interfere," Larry said to the pastor. "It's just their way of showing their love."

The pastor decided to test the love. "What would happen, Larry, if you did resist them?"

Larry cringed. "I don't think either I or they could take it."

"Their love has its limits, then: it depends on your not crossing them," the pastor pointed out.

Although the fear of opposing a parent or parents is based on a fear of their rejection, the commandment to honor them reenforces this fear. If Larry seems open to further dialoguing, the pastor may point out that honoring them in terms of his marital vows means also to leave them (Gen. 2:24). Honoring parents as an adult does not mean being obedient like a child. There is wisdom in the principle that one must first leave father and mother before one can cleave to a mate. The goal of counseling, in this instance, is to catalyze a maturing process that has long been overdo. Larry needs support to be firm with his parents.

"While your parents are going to be shaken up if you affirm your marital priority and may even 'pull out all the stops' to make you feel guilty," the pastor said, "I believe they will learn in time to adjust to their new roles."

"I hope so," Larry said, "but if not I will have to accept that too. The test will come this weekend when I inform them that we won't be taking our vacation with them as usual at their cottage this year."

Larry did not arrive at this conclusion after one session of counseling. Pastoral counselors need the virtue of patience. It takes time—even with the dialogical approach—to penetrate the entrenched defenses of what are basically frightened people. As Paul said, "I planted, Apollos watered, but God gave the growth" (1 Cor. 3:6). In these role rigidities the pastor sows the seeds of change. The pastor and/or his or her successor may water the soil. The breakthrough occurs when the Spirit who speaks through the Word gives the growth. The counselor also "waits on the Lord."

Uncomfortable for Good Reason

The authority of the pastor in the use of the Scripture respects the "space" of the counselee. The dialogical approach is itself a protection against trespassing on another's freedom. Even though the pastor does not misuse his or her authority, however, some persons may project their own distorted image of authority into the dialogue. They may "feel" the pastor's judgment, though he or she has not communicated it—even nonverbally. Any reference to moral or religious values may make such a person feel uncomfortable, and he may protest by saying, "Now you are laying a guilt trip on me!" Although it takes time to change this image of authority in the other's mind, the pastor's modeling of another kind of authority will begin to create its own impression. To facilitate the change, the pastor may explain his intentions: "My purpose was not to make you feel guilty, but to inquire into your own thoughts about the moral issues in this problem."

One may feel uncomfortable in the presence of an authority figure when moral and religious values are discussed, not only because of one's dated images of authority, but also because one is guilty in one's *own* eyes. Although there are many ways of distracting ourselves from our own self-judgment, the presence of religious symbols tends to resurrect it. We then project this self-judgment onto the authority figure and interpret what he or she says accordingly. The pastor's purpose in these matters, however, is to provide the counselees with encouragement to listen to their own inner voices—all of them—and to own them. Counseling can help one to come to terms with one's inner polarities.

As a healing ministry, pastoral counseling tends to focus on the aesthetic level of perception—with how the person *feels*. But there is a moral and ethical level to pastoral counseling also. To feel better on any lasting basis one may also have to *do* better. Behavioral changes, however, often involve moral choices. Religiously speaking, these choices are vocational choices. If one is not one's own, then these choices are a response to the call of God. They are acts of obedience—of commitment.

Counselors, including pastoral counselors, are reluctant to foist their values onto the counselee, and rightly so. Pastoral counselors, however, represent a particular tradition that involves a commitment to a way of life. While there is much flexibility within this way, there are nevertheless also explicit parameters. In a view of life in which one is not one's own, there are vocational responsibilities. These are inherent in any ministry of the church, including pastoral counseling. Commitment to vocational responsibilities, therefore, is a legitimate concern of the pastoral counselor.

Commitment to something beyond your own well-being is not the "in thing" in our day. As noted previously, our emphasis, instead, is on the search for our own fulfillment. Our concern is with feeling good, and we are not too interested in the future consequences of this enjoyment. Such shortsighted gratification is taking a heavy toll on our intimate relationships and on our health. Whether one wants to think about the future or not, in the irreversible movement of time the future is soon the present.

As those who have been "bought with a price," we have obligations beyond the satisfaction of our own desires. Divorce, for example, is not simply a personal or even a family matter. The Marriage Encounter Movement reminds each couple that all the Marriage Encounter couples have a stake in their marriage. Even on a secular basis, self-indulgence undermines the interdependency in which we live. The reluctance to sacrifice for the common good during the energy crisis is an example of its destructive influence. As creatures under God we are called to care for one another. At times such care may involve the sacrifice of our immediate desires and satisfactions.

In pastoral care and counseling the question of what one is doing with one's life is of central importance. In the choices that lie before us in plotting our life's direction, we need to raise not only the aesthetic questions but also the moral and religious ones. The pastor's care for the counselee is shown in his or her courage to raise such issues. What the counselee does with them is not the counselor's responsibility, but if he or she raises them dialogically, the experience may revive the counselee's own inner response to them.

Use of Scripture for Devotional Support

The Scripture is also a resource in pastoral counseling for "homework." Carl Rogers suggested homework for the counselee in one of his early books, and since then TA, Reality Therapy, Systems Counseling, and others have expanded the concept to include many and varied exercises, contracts, and transactions. Pastoral counseling offers a unique form of this homework in the practice of personal devotions. Although personal devotions is an old Christian tradition, it also corresponds to contemporary forms for meditation. Although meditation is currently associated primarily with Eastern religions, the Christian faith has its own meditational heritage. This heritage belongs to the pastoral counseling ministry. It can be taught and practiced, for example, in the counseling session.

Meditation is the type of homework that can develop into a daily discipline throughout one's life. I have a psychiatrist friend who teaches his clients to meditate as a secular exercise. He reasons that if his clients are not willing to invest twenty minutes a day into their healing, they are not very serious about getting well. In pastoral counseling the relationship goes beyond a relation to the counselor to a relationship with God. According to a theology of the universal priesthood, the pastor is a counselor to priests—or at least to potential priests. Assigning homework in meditation and prayer is a support to this priestly capacity of the counselee for the divine–human encounter. In meditation one learns to become still so that one may listen to the Word of God. "Be still, and know that I am God" (Psalm 46:10). Knowing who *God* is helps us also to know who *we* are. It is this identification that leads to our sense of vocation.

In meditation the emphasis is on the interrelationship of mind, body, and spirit. The exercise begins with bodily relaxation as a prelude to mental receptivity and spiritual experience. As a clinical placement in my graduate training I was assigned to the Class in Thought Control conducted by Dr. Joseph B. Pratt at the Boston Dispensary. For this weekly class Pratt gathered specific patients from his dispensary whose health problems were largely psychosomatic. He taught them how to relax their bodies and minds much like the teachers of meditation do today. Since that time I have used this "healing" exercise for myself and as a resource in my pastoral counseling, coupling it, as did Pratt, with biblical content. The conscious relaxing of the body and slowing of the mind clears away obstacles to our listening to the Spirit of God.

The cognitive content for Christian meditation has traditionally come primarily from the Bible. With the concentration of the total person, one listens to the Word. As a symbol of communication the Word is not only something we hear but also something we see. It stimulates our imagination to picture in our mind what we cannot as yet see in the world. Meditation has been called "focused imagination," and in Christian meditation the Bible is the stimulus for this focus. In meditation one listens not only with the rational mind, but with the mind that includes the "heart."

When I guide a counselee in meditation, I attempt to select Scripture that is pertinent to his or her needs. I quote a verse or describe a story or parable and then leave time for silent reflection. As Henri Nouwen says, "Silence opens in us the space where the word can be heard." I begin the exercise as did Pratt by directing the body to relax, starting with the toes and working up to the head. I then direct the mind to slow its pace and suggest that it imagine a scene that to it symbolizes peace. The selected Scripture may then follow as content for continuing visualization and reflection. I begin this part of the meditation by saying, "In the presence of God we listen now to his Word."

Following the scriptural portion, I move into prayer by directing the counselee to express his or her petitions visually; for example, to see oneself breaking free from one's destructive ways and doing things differently and constructively. This "picture petitioning" can be expanded into intercession for significant others. Each petition is also interspersed by moments for silent reflection. The counselee may wish to tape the guided meditation as a help in getting started in his or her devotional homework. One should be encouraged, however, in the process of time to develop one's own personalized style. (For a more detailed description of the meditation process I refer to my book on the subject, *Let the Spirit In,* Abingdon, 1979.)

The discipline of meditation is a stabilizing and integrating influence, conducive to our spiritual growth. In the meditative tradition the practice is called *centering*—getting into focus—locating our spiritual center of gravity. The meditator is positioning—conditioning oneself to take responsibility for one's life. Meditation is a way of reenforcing our identity as sons and daughters of God—of knowing who we are by knowing *whose* we are. It is a counteractive to the stresses that disintegrate our self-direction.

As we have seen, meditation moves easily into prayer. In listening to the Word one is already in communication with God. But prayer as a resource in pastoral counseling is a subject in itself, and it is to this subject that we now turn.

Summary

The Bible is a specific resource in pastoral care and counseling because it brings the Word of God to the needs of people. As a means for the Spirit's communication with the human spirit, the Bible can be used to free people from inhibiting pieties so that their dialogue with the Spirit can accommodate *all* of their feelings. Because it is an authority symbol, pastors and others have at times misused the Bible to stifle rather than to encourage this free expression. With the gamut of emotions from despair and hostility to joy and elation expressed in the Psalms as well as in other sections of Scripture, the obvious answer to such misuse is not disuse but proper use. This same liberating influence can be used in clarifying distortions concerning marital and family roles. At the same time biblical descriptions of one's commitment or vocation as a child of God are also resources in pastoral care and counseling. One's personal integration, Christianly speaking, is connected with one's commitment.

Because of this multifaceted nature of the Scripture, the criteria for its use in pastoral care and counseling depends upon the pastor's awareness of the counselee's need together with what use of the Bible would be a helpful resource in this instance. When the counselee is particularly tense, frightened, defeated or otherwise upset, the meditative use of Scripture may be especially helpful. Such devotional meditation can be a form of homework to assist in the healing of memories as well as in the changing of behavior. The openness of the counselee to this or other uses of the Bible is another criterion which the pastor needs to ascertain. Discussing the option with the counselee will frequently reveal whether he or she is ready for the resource. The pastor needs to accept a negative response without viewing it as a personal rejection.

7

Prayer
in Pastoral Counseling

In *Understanding Prayer* Edgar Jackson says that he is "inclined to think that the benefits of counseling might not be necessary if there were a more adequate prayer life practiced by persons who were trying to find their way in life." Since an "adequate prayer life" is a possible preventative of the need for counseling, prayer as a resource in pastoral counseling is also a way of helping persons carry on after counseling. Our concern in this chapter, however, is the use of prayer *during* pastoral care and counseling. We shall focus on the reasons for using this resource and the criteria for when and how to use it.

Prayer as a Response

Prayer is first of all a resource for the *pastor*. Intercessory prayers are an important part of the ministry of pastoral care and counseling. I use the meditative form of prayer in intercession for my counselees, picturing them in this milieu as growing, coping, and affirming life. While such prayer is not a substitute for counseling, it is an undergirding support for the counseling and for the counselee.

Although it would appear that in prayer we are taking the initiative, prayer is actually a response to God's initiative. In meditation, prayer is a response to listening to the Word—to the Spirit's speaking. This Word contains the invitation to prayer. Prayer is presented in the Scripture as a way by which we share with God and work together with him. It is the dialogical exercise of the relationship which God has established with us through Christ. Such prayer includes petition. In fact, the lack of such petitioning is given as a reason for our not receiving. "You do not have because you do not ask" (James 4:2). Jesus' words put it in the positive: "Ask, and it will be given you" (Matt. 7:7).

Yet one can ask *wrongly,* says James, and *not* receive. This happens when we desire to "spend" what we receive "on our passions," that is, when we use prayer as an attempt to manipulate God into satisfying our self-centered desires (James 4:3). Some are reluctant to ask anything for themselves since *any* such asking seems selfish. We can ask *rightly,* however as well as *wrongly.* It is of legitimate self-concern to ask for health, for guidance, and for the ability to direct ourselves, for example. Actually we cannot manipulate God, even though we try. Those who ask "wrongly" do not receive. Therefore, we can afford to err on the side of asking rather than not asking, trusting our petitions to his love and wisdom.

In using prayer as a resource in pastoral care and counseling, we pray for another and at the same time assist the other to pray. As an expression of intimacy in a relationship comparable in both Testaments to marriage, prayer can take various forms. Communication between mates also has many forms. In Marriage Encounter, for instance, mates are instructed in a particular form for written and verbal dialogues. So also in our marriage with God there is always the possibility for more effective forms of prayer. Like all analogies, this one limps. Marriage is between two finite and fallible human beings, while our relationship with God is with the One who is the "Wholly Other." Prayer brings to our consciousness the presence of the living God with all the mystery of the *numi-*

nous. God is personal, but also supra-personal: he is more than a being; he is Being itself. Consequently the pastor needs to be sensitive to the counselee's readiness for a resource that assumes the presence of God in awesome encounter.

There is a variety of forms for prayer. We have already described the mental picture communication of meditation. Most of these forms, however, use words. In the pastor's use of prayer in pastoral care and counseling, these words are expressed audibly rather than by mere lip movement or by remaining unspoken in thought. In the verbalization of prayer there are also variant forms. One may offer a free prayer or use a formal prayer. Free prayer, however, is only "free" from a prescribed liturgical form; it has its own particular structure, depending on the person or the group who uses it. In pastoral praying one needs to take into account the religious background of the other; one feels more secure with familiar forms in approaching the deity.

Whether free or formal, the wording of prayer in the counseling process is existential—of the moment—prayer. Even when formal prayers are used, they are selected on the basis of the need of the moment. I often close a guided meditation with a formal prayer such as the following collect.

> Grant us, O Lord, for our spiritual growth, thoughts that pass into prayers, prayers that pass into love, and love that passes into eternal life, through Jesus Christ our Lord.

Traditional forms such as those associated with public worship, festivals, and celebrations enrich our religious experience. The use of a familiar hymn, for instance, spoken in conjunction with prayer, can stimulate the memories associated with it. This is particularly true for older people who often need a tie with their religious past to perceive meaning in their present apparently purposeless existence. The same, of course, is true in our family relationships and celebrations when the repetition of the traditional family forms enhances the experience of intimacy.

Yet these forms do not constitute the essence of this intimacy. They are expressions of it and are meaningful only as symbols of a shared life because there *is* a shared life. Consequently these forms need to be used in tension with spontaneity so that the new and the vital is not stifled by traditional ways. Without this balance, prescribed forms can be obstacles to, rather than expressions of, intimacy. The cry, "Lord, save me!" for example, creates its own form in the existential moment. I have been moved at times to offer such prayers pastorally in identification with a sufferer's anguish.

In spite of the plea for change explicit in existential prayer, our prayers are also our response to a spiritual order inherent in our new nature. They are verbalized attempts to affirm or to restore our identification with our Source, our Center. As Edgar Jackson puts it, our prayers are petitions for release from the increasing self-consciousness that surrounds us in our pains, to see instead the windows of God-consciousness that disclose the larger vision of our journey. Prayer then is our attempt to maintain our spirit on the same wave length with the witnessing Spirit of God (Rom. 8:16).

Mediatorial Role

The use of prayer as a resource in pastoral care and counseling is in harmony with the pastor's symbolic role in the ministry of the church. He or she is, in a sense, a mediator, articulator, intercessor, between a world limited to sense and time and a world of faith where "with God all things are possible" (Matt. 19:26). In bridging these two worlds the pastor is a symbol at that moment of the Incarnation, in which these worlds are united in Christ. In this mediatorial role pastoral prayer becomes a focal use of God-talk by which one *talks* with God. In praying aloud with the counselee the pastor is using the resource that bridges in our consciousness the world that is limited with the world that is unlimited. It is the activity that expresses, as well as affirms, a creative tension between the finite and the infinite.

While the symbolic role is focused on the ordained clergy, the laity are also priests who may function pastorally in their ministry to others. In this sense the incarnation is communicated through *all* of the members of the body of Christ. Those who are ordained are specifically entrusted by the body with the supervision of this ministry. The pastoral counselor, for example, depending upon the specific nature of the relationship, may encourage the counselee also to pray aloud in the counseling session to enhance the shared experience. Other helping professionals, as well as society as a whole, seem content to leave this mediatorial use of prayer to the pastoral counselor. While laypersons in these professions may on occasion use prayer, they do so for reasons other than the nature of their professions. In pastoral care and counseling, the consensus is that prayer is a resource that belongs organically to the profession.

This role identification with prayer has been abused by both pastors and those to whom they minister. Some people seem to believe that the pastor has not really functioned as a pastor unless he or she prays with them, regardless of how personally significant their dialogue may otherwise be. Some pastors may believe likewise. This rigidity or stereotyping, of the pastoral encounter has the effect of downplaying the importance of the dialogue that takes place. In fact, some may ask the pastor to pray in order to keep from engaging in any significant dialogue, and some pastors may look to prayer to redeem an otherwise sterile encounter. When this happens, prayer becomes a means for keeping the two worlds separated, and the religion involved remains unincarnated. The pastor achieves a special status that removes him or her from this world—a professional image that is apart from the common dialogue. The pastor's function then is one of division rather than mediation, and his or her praying, a mark of the separated worlds.

Because of this abuse and also as a resistance against such separation from the world, other pastors may have the opposite problem. They find it difficult to pray for *any* reason. Praying itself seems to remove them from the common life, and they feel uncomfortably artificial in doing it. Unless the person specifically asks them to pray, they will probably not do so. Unfortunately they are neglecting a powerful resource which they among all other helping professionals are uniquely qualified and designated to use. As with God-talk and Scripture, disuse of prayer may be a temporary reaction to abuse, but eventually the only satisfying answer is positive use. We need to be emancipated from compulsions either to pray or not to pray so that we can be alert to the Spirit's guidance in the existential moment.

The needs of the person rather than the pastor's predispositions should determine the nature of the pastor's ministry. The decision regarding the use of prayer should be based on this principle. Is prayer a resource that is applicable at this time with this person? Has the movement of the dialogue indicated a need for it? Although a person is religiously-oriented, he or she may not desire the pastor's assistance in praying. By the same token, one may have no particular need for the pastor's assistance in praying, but may have a desire for a *corporate* experience in prayer. If the pastor has any doubt about where the counselee is in regard to these questions, he or she can ask. In fact, I believe it is wise to ask even when one has decided that prayer is in order. I have been surprised at times to have a person decline the offer when I had thought he or she would affirm it. To lead a person reluctantly into prayer is ill-advised. I would prefer to know the person's wishes in advance.

Prayer and One's Image of God

Since stress situations are the occasion for most of our pastoral praying, the use of prayer raises the question of who is this God to whom we call for help? What is his responsibility in the discrepancies and distresses of life? What sort of power does he possess to relieve them? Some people seem to find help in accepting their troubles as the will of God. The line of authority is then clear, and their course is to adjust. Others recoil from this interpretation, refusing to identify God's intent with their pain. These are more likely to question or to protest their misfortune. Still others find help by believing that God *accepts* rather than *wills* their adversities. It is difficult to arrive at a theodicy that satisfies when one has suffered inexplicable reverses. Though we are God's people, we live in a fallen world and are not spared the adversities that are common to it. Job in his agony sought desperately for a reason. Why should he, a righteous man, suffer such misfortune? Who or what is responsible? If God isn't "running the show," who is? And if God *is* in charge, why the tragedies?

Christians differ on this question, even as there are differing emphases in the Bible. The "answer" that satisfies is probably based as much on one's own personal understanding of what is reasonable—which in turn is based on one's past experiences and individual nature—as on any profound theological insight that can be universalized. Yet, if we are to remain within a Christian frame of reference, there are parameters in our search for a satisfying answer. Any view of providence that by-passes or even minimizes the tragic dimensions of life is by-passing a theology of the cross. Such a view may be positive, but it is not empathic. I know from my own experience as a counselee that those who can deal with tragedy only by pointing out the positive side of things do not touch base with the sufferer.

On the other hand, any view that confines providence to God's empathy bypasses a theology of victory. The impotency of this God moves his ministers to pray with timid and generalized petitions. One can take no risks in praying because one's God has no power. In contrast, Kierkegaard defines God as the "one for whom all things are possible—every instant." The Christian message in any crisis situation is that God is *involved*. He is incarnated in human stress, although the stress situation may "hide" his presence. We then have a problem over what appears to be his absence. Though Christ died in apparent impotency, he rose in power from the dead. There are no limits to grace, no end to surprises. The faith that is expressed by prayer—and energized through praying—is the recipient of this grace. In praying, one forms a partnership with *mystery*. The implicit element of surprise is probably a factor in our interest in living.

This leads to the question, what is the purpose of prayer in situations of stress? The obvious answer is, to facilitate healing —of body, mind, spirit, in marital and family relationships. We can interpret this facilitation in magical terms as did a patient stricken with serious illness. In attempting to ascertain where she was religiously, I asked if she had found prayer helpful in her stress. "It helped before," she said, "but not this time."

"How is that?" I asked.

"Well, the last time when I was real sick, I prayed and I got well. This time I prayed and I'm not getting well."

Obviously her purpose in praying was now exhausted, unless one could persuade her to try once more. "This time it might work!"

Her view of prayer was limited enough and needed no such pastoral reenforcing. Instead, her comment provided the opportunity to dialogue with her about prayer and about God's involvement in her life. The prayer to facilitate healing is more than an impersonal asking and receiving. It is not simply a way of getting rid of our pain; it is also a way of providing meaning in the midst of our pain. Prayer is an activity that has its own good effects on our lives. It is a means for staying in touch with our Creator when the stressful situation tends to make us feel separated, alienated, and alone. As any activity productive of spiritual growth, prayer is far more than a primitive attempt to persuade the deity on our behalf. God's invitation to us to pray becomes our initiative. Prayer, then, is actually more than a human activity; it is a happening, and God is doing it as much as we.

When we pray, we are not implying that the resources for our healing are external to us. Although God is the Wholly Other, he is also the one who dwells within us. As our Creator he has endowed our bodies with disease-resisting antibodies, and our minds with reason so that we may cope with reality rather than evade or distort it. Our marital and family relationships also have inherent within them specific strengths that are resources for healing, even though they may be eclipsed at troubled times by obvious weaknesses. These inherent means for restoration need to be acknowledged and encouraged. Our prayers actually are a reenforcement of them.

The biblical focus in our being created in God's image is that we are made for communion with the Creator. "Our hearts are restless, O God, until they find their rest in thee (Augustine). Prayer is an exercise of this communion and therefore a means for affirming our identity. To live as redeemed creatures in a fallen world we need to "walk by faith and not by sight" (2 Cor. 5:7). Faith is the stance for wholeness—the means for receiving health and salvation. Prayer is an expression, an exercise, a stimulation of this faith. God is not being "pressured" by our prayers. Rather, he is out in front of us, beckoning us to respond to him so that we can receive what he desires to give. Since our prayer is really our response to God's overture, I often conclude my pastoral prayers with the petition, "Help us to be open to receive that for which we pray." Directed as it is to God, our prayer aligns us with our

Source and therefore with the resources for our health and wholeness.

An initial obstacle to prayer in stress situations may be one's misgivings over why one should be so afflicted. The *why* is a protest, not a question for information. It is the Jobian protest. In her work with the terminally ill Kübler-Ross has observed that this protest needs to be faced and expressed before one may accept his or her dying. "Those who have the courage to scream and rage, if necessary, to question God, to share their pain and agony are the ones whose faces were peaceful and radiant when they left." The protest may be one's only genuine response at the moment to what is happening in one's life. It may be the way the afflicted have to take in order to arrive at a satisfying understanding of God's place in their affliction. As Nouwen says, the protest needs to be "converted into prayer." Like Job one "utters" what one "did not understand" (Job 42:3), but it is an authentic utterance and a needed step *toward* understanding.

The protest may itself be a prayer if it is directed toward God. It may even be contained in "sighs too deep for words," by which the Spirit intercedes for us (Rom. 8:26). Nevertheless, one may not recognize it as prayer because one's understanding of prayer does not include protest. In counseling with a man who was frustrated over his failure to advance in his work and the subsequent problems this was creating in his family, I inquired into his openness to receiving help from his religious faith. "I'm not ready to pray," he said. "I guess I'm too bitter." I suggested that he might share his bitterness with God—that I was confident that God could take it. "That's foreign to me," he said. "I just can't see myself being religious about bitterness."

I pointed to a chair beside him. "Imagine God in that chair," I said. "Now tell him what you are thinking—what you are feeling." I knew it would be difficult, but I believed he would try. He began haltingly, but with encouragement he finally directed his resentment to the chair. "I don't understand why you don't help me—why you let things happen that really aren't fair." When he finished he said, "Now you see why I can't pray."

"That was prayer," I said. "You were sharing what is going on inside of you with God." His protest was a toned down version of Job's. "Does it seem good to thee to oppress, to despise the work of thy hands and favor the design of the wicked? . . . Thy hands fashioned and made me; and now thou dost turn about and destroy me" (Job 10:3, 8). Since our relationship to God is comparable to a marital relationship, such prayers are like lovers' quarrels. The conflicts need to be worked through so that a renewed and deepened understanding may result.

We have been emphasizing the use of words in prayer. Obviously, God does not need our words to hear us; rather it is we who may need to use words in order to pray. Words are our chief symbol of communication; they are the means by which we share with one another and know one another. It is only natural for us to use words when we share with God, even though we know rationally that God, as Tennyson says, is "closer than breathing and nearer than hands and feet."

Words are basic also to our knowing God. In speaking to us through his Word, God uses words to reveal himself. There is consequently a natural coupling of this Word and prayer, our words being a response to his words. In my own pastoral praying I use Scripture and prayer interchangeably as an expression of this response. The following is an example of such a prayer, used as a resource in a marital crisis.

> Father, we come to you in our distress, for you have bidden us to come to you in the day of trouble and you will hear us. Help our marriage. Give us the strength to endure the pressures of the ordeal. Help us in moments of stress to be open to your guidance so that what we say and do may not hinder your good purposes. Forgive us when we may have hindered. You have prom-

ised that if we confess our sins, you are faithful and just to forgive our sins, for the blood of Jesus Christ cleanses us from all sin. Help us to give the love to others that you have first given to us. Touch our hearts —husband and wife—that both may be open to your guidance. May the present crisis in our marriage be so resolved that we may be closer to each other than before. We pray this confidently because we pray in Jesus' name.

A similar example for use in depression and loss of direction.

"Now abideth faith, hope and love." O God, restore us to hope. When our feelings become too much for us, help us to hear the invitation of your Son, "Come unto me, all you that labor and are heavy laden, and I will give you rest." We are grateful that "he was tempted in all points like as we are," for this means that you understand how we feel. But you seem so far away at times, God. "I believe—but help my unbelief." Lord, you are here. Help us to realize your presence. Give us confidence to believe that you are working your ways even now, though we do not see your hand. In the name of "him who died for us and rose again." Amen.

There are times when other forms of communication may accompany prayer. The ministry of touch is one example. When praying with those in the sick bed or in crisis situations, the pastor may hold the hand or lay his or her hand on the shoulder or the head of the person. God's care is "incarnated" in the physical touch of a caring person. The touch is an encouragement to trust as one prays. I was present when the pastor called on my bereaved father shortly after the funeral of my mother. After they talked about his loss and about their life of over fifty years together, the pastor in parting embraced my father, holding him in a gesture of empathy. The pastor's embrace was a symbol of the embrace of God which my father needed to support him in his devastating loss.

The Holy Communion is another example of communication that is supportive to prayer. The tangible elements of the sacrament, together with its drama of redemption, may be the reenforcement that some need in order to pray. In counseling with a man overwhelmed by fear because he believed he was doomed to fail, I sensed that though he was open to the idea of prayer, he was emotionally closed to the hope that prayer implies. Perhaps the sacrament could be a means for breaking through this obstacle of panic. I inquired concerning his interest. Upon receiving his consent, I prepared the "table" as I narrated the story of the institution of the sacrament. The man's involvement in the drama and his participation with me in the eating and drinking of the elements proved helpful in penetrating his foreboding. When we closed with a prayer specific to his problem, he was able to join in the hope for healing.

Prayer Grows Out of the Dialogue

The resource of prayer in pastoral counseling is organically related to the counseling dialogue. As prayer opens a person to receive, so the counseling process removes obstacles to openness. Prayer, then, is the natural climax to some pastoral dialogues, and is not simply a concluding addition to these dialogues. *Knowing* in counseling precedes *praying* in counseling. As a pastor perceives a person's needs as these are revealed in the session, he or she is in a position to articulate these needs in intercession to God.

The pastoral dialogue is a sharing experience in which the message is "let it out." Pastors, therefore, need to discipline themselves to listen to what comes out. When more is revealed than the pastor had anticipated, his or her defenses may be activated. Knowing that one can share it together in prayer may lower these defenses: the pastor is not alone. This is not an escapist consolation—although it can be so misused —but rather it is a realistic awareness of *who* God is. The anticipation that one can "share the load" with God in prayer, far from being a substitute for coming to terms with difficult matters, is a support for this undertaking. Prayer, therefore, is a resource in pastoral counseling for meeting the counselor's needs as well as those of the counselee.

Since the activity of prayer grows out of the pastoral dialogue, the dialogue and the prayer are of one piece. When concerns are shared during the session and the prayer reflects these concerns, its occurrence is natural rather than forced. The content of the prayer, as well as the form in which it is offered, is adapted to the counselee's *story*. At the conclusion of a presurgical visit a pastor asked the patient—to whom he had been referred by a friend—if he desired prayer. The patient replied, "I only know one prayer."

"Is it the Lord's prayer?" the pastor asked.

The patient replied by saying, "Lord, grant me the serenity to accept the things that I cannot change, the courage to change the things I can, and the wisdom to know the difference."

"AA," said the pastor.

"Right," said the patient.

"Your surgery is an attempt to change something," said the pastor, "so let's pray for it in that way—for God's guidance for your surgeon, and for his healing power for your body."

"I'd like that," said the patient.

The pastor's prayer was a way of commiting the surgery to the "Higher Power."

Prayer in Jesus' Name

In AA the Higher Power is "God as we understand him." The Christian understands him as he is revealed in Christ. Prayer in a Christian perspective, consequently, is offered "in

Jesus' name." Some have used these words legalistically, imply-ing that if the words are not spoken, the prayer is not valid. In interfaith gatherings their insistence on the "words" is a mistaken understanding of fidelity, and leads those of other than Christian persuasions to feel excluded, if not "put down." The phrase also can degenerate into an empty ritual. This, of course, is the risk of all forms of expression.

The phrase itself is pertinent to prayer since it is through Christ we have "access in one Spirit to the Father" (Eph. 2:18). As Peter put it, "Lord, to whom shall we go? You have the words of eternal life" (John 6:68). The boundaries of the im-possible are penetrated by his access. We have our limits, and often they are painfully clear. Yet if we have no vision that penetrates these limits, we will end up in despair. At the same time, the vision of possibility has to remain in tension with our limits; otherwise we will end up in the despair of fantasy. As Kierkegaard has pointed out, it is only by living with this dialectic between our limits and our possibilities that we can be both realistic and hopeful. "In Jesus' Name" is a theological expression of this dialectic.

Do I have the right to pray? Do I deserve to be healed? These are questions that are resolved by the Good News of our reconciliation. "In Jesus' name" means we can "with con-fidence draw near to the throne of grace"—that we are invited to ask—that we "may receive mercy and find grace to help in time of need" (Heb. 4:16).

We need this encouragement to ask. The pastor may also lack it. I can vividly recall an instance which revealed my own lack of it. An 86-year-old woman was awaiting an operation that would supply her with the first of two new hips. She was anticipating being able once again to "get around" before she died. However I was met in the hall by her son who somberly informed me that the surgeon decided against the operation because tests had indicated a possible cancerous condition in her abdomen. I entered her room expecting to find her depressed. Instead she was somewhat indignant. "I don't have cancer!" she said. After we talked about the surgeon's decision and her disappointment, I concluded, as in my previous visits, with prayer. Discomfited by the disappointing news, I petitioned in generalized terms that were so broad that even I was not sure for what I was praying. I suppose I told myself I did not want to engender any false hopes. But how could I know which hope would be false?

When I finished, she pointed a finger at me and said, "You didn't pray for my new hips!"

I felt impaled. "You're right," I said. "Let's do it again." This time I prayed for her new hips.

I probably would have forgotten the incident except that three months later she was back for her operation.

"I told you I didn't have cancer," she said. She received her first new hip with few complications, and subsequently her second. She had encouraged a timid pastor to ask that she might receive.

We are afraid of "getting out on a limb" in our pastoral prayers. So we pray *safely*. Under the guise of "protecting God," we fail in fulfilling our own responsibility in our relationship to him. Our petitions are not demands on God; they are not tests of our faith or risks to our own reputation. Nor are they attempts to manipulate the universe: direct asking is not manipulation. Our responsibility is to affirm life, figuratively as well as literally, even though death with all of its symbols is all about us. Our petitions are an expression of this affirmation. Yet these same petitions "let God be God." We stay out of his responsibility, even as we fulfill our own. Besides being a way of meeting our responsibility, prayer is also an inspiration to believe and to hope. By taking the leap of faith in our asking, we are stimulating that faith in its openness to receive.

Although we have referred to prayer as a climax to some pastoral encounters, the pastoral dialogue may need to continue after the prayer. Our praying does not "create" the presence of God, but it is a help to us in realizing this presence. The effect of this realization differs, of course, with persons. For some, it breaks down their emotional controls, and nonverbal expressions of deep feelings may be quite evident. Instead of leaving after the prayer, the pastor may respond to the nonverbal communication either by some affectionate touch or verbally as well. "Do you want to say what you are feeling?" The response will indicate whether or not the person desires more from the pastor. At least one has had the opportunity. Usually the feelings that come with prayer are those associated with intimacy—with feeling cared for and loved.

But not always. The effect can also be negative. A pastor shared with me his concern about a hospital patient with whom he had prayed, but who informed him immediately upon his return visit that he did not want him to pray again. The pastor was taken aback by the firmness of the request and assented with a minimum of words. But the incident bothered him, and he wanted to discuss it. My assumption was that the patient felt coerced into prayer, that he was unprepared for the effect it had on him, and wanted no more of it. The pastor might have picked up the resistance prior to praying by asking if the man wanted prayer and then taking seriously both the verbal and nonverbal response. A reply like, "It's OK if *you* want to," for example, is not exactly an affirmation. He also might have picked up the negative effect had he been sensitive to the nonverbal communication after the prayer.

He had an additional opportunity to discuss this effect at the next visit when he received the request for no more prayer, but he was too affected himself by the request to do so. Suppose, instead, that he had responded by saying, "Of course. The choice of prayer is yours to make—not mine. But I am interested in your request. Evidently our prayer last time was not what you really wanted." This would give the patient the opportunity to go into the matter if he desired, and the pastor may not have remained so much in the dark about what happened. Even more important, the question may have initiated a significant dialogue on where this man was—or wasn't—religiously.

Instruction in Prayer

Besides being a form of intercession, prayer in pastoral care and counseling is an instruction in prayer. Even in our churches many people feel inadequate in prayer and desire help with their spiritual life, even though they may not openly request it. The disciples of Jesus spoke for more than themselves when they said, "Lord, teach us to pray." When one prays aloud within the dialogical milieu, one is teaching the other to pray, if such teaching is desired. Since the content of the prayer is based on the existential need that one has shared, the directing of this sharing in intercession to God is an effective way to teach and to learn.

Such prayers may be stormy as well as calm. There is a difference, for example, between the incident mentioned above, when Jesus taught his disciples what is now known as the Lord's Prayer, and his prayers in the Garden of Gethsemane on the night of his betrayal. The disciples could have learned about prayer that night also had they watched and prayed with him as he requested, rather than going to sleep. If they had realized their danger, there would have been no sleeping.

In like manner the pastor teaches people how to pray when he prays with them in their situations of stress. Emerging from the pastoral dialogue, these prayers can be specific rather than generalized, to the point rather than in clichés and standardized phrases. Since the counselee is deeply involved in the dialogue, he is likely also to be deeply involved in the expression of this dialogue in prayer.

Teaching to pray is actually teaching a way of life. The prayer "channel" is always open: there is the moment-by-moment potential for communion. Through prayer we can get in touch with our Center. In formulating our petitions we are moved to clarify our thinking concerning what it is we want. Prayer leads to knowing—ourselves, and thereby also our neighbor and God. It is a way of focusing on our spiritual center—of being in tune with the Eternal Spirit—of maintaining our equilibrium in a fallen world.

Prayer is also related to other forms of communication, such as the ministry of touch—the laying on of hands—and the sacrament of Holy Communion. We turn now to these other forms as they are integrated within the larger resource of the congregation.

Summary

As with the resources of God-talk and Scripture, the resource of prayer is used in pastoral care and counseling when dynamics of the relationship so indicate. A favorable context would consist not only of the need of the counselee for the support of prayer but also of his or her openness to it. The pastor enters that context also with his or her own predispositions regarding prayer, which must be taken into account along with these other factors. The purpose of prayer in this ministry is to engage the relationship existentially with the Presence of God. Through the medium of petitioning, one's trust in God can be directed to needs revealed in the counseling process. One's image of God not only determines how one perceives such petitioning, but also how one perceives the entire purpose of prayer. Consequently, dialoguing about this image prior to prayer is sometimes helpful in counteracting the frequent misuse of this resource. Prayers that grow out of the counseling dialogue are organically related to the pastoral counseling process with its orientation to a system that includes not only the counselor-counselee relationship, but also the relationship of each to God.

8

The Congregation:
A Worshiping, Fellowshiping, Healing, Witnessing Community

Pastoral care and counseling is not something in and of itself, since the pastor is a pastor of a congregation. Chaplains in institutions do not have congregations in the usual sense, but they still have a corporate ministry that involves the other disciplines besides pastoral care and counseling. They often also serve as leaders of a worship community within the institution. Pastors associated with denominational social services or medical clinics also do not serve congregations, but are often supported by congregations and relate their ministry to congregations. As a community of faith the congregation—or parish— is of vital significance to the pastoral care and counseling ministry, a resource to which the pastor's counselees need to be exposed. It may help to explain to some counselees how the pastor's counseling ministry is related to his or her total ministry with and to the congregation. Pastors can with good reason encourage their counselees' involvement in the life of a congregation so that they may receive the ministry of the church in its totality. This will in turn enhance what they are receiving through the counseling ministry.

Edgar Jackson entitled his book on pastoral counseling, *Parish Counseling* because he believes that the religious resources of the counselor focus at the point where the pastor functions "in the unique social institution called the parish." The parish milieu shapes the pastoral care and counseling ministry. Even in so-called private practice, pastoral counseling needs this connection with the life of a parish to be pastoral in the full significance of the word. The pastor is ordained by the body of Christ, the body of believers, to minister to them, with them, and for them. In turn, this body itself is a resource in this pastoral ministry.

Room for Development

There is much room for development in the use of this resource. The congregation as a local community of faith is the most unused, undeveloped, and unorganized of all the unique resources of the pastoral counselor. Pastoral counseling has been influenced by the medical or professional model, in which the professional, as an individual, works alone or in the company of other professionals in the sufficiency of a professional team. There is too much emphasis in the congregation on the pastor's ministering *to* the people of the congregation and *for* them—and too little on *with* them. Without the congregation's ministry *with* the pastor, his or her counseling ministry is hampered. It is lacking the concrete embodiment of the resources which are distinctly pastoral in nature. It is also deficient in the integration or connection between the various pastoral functions that is potentially inherent in a total congregational ministry.

The congregation as a community of faith is a resource for pastoral counseling in its various community dimensions. It is first of all a *worshiping* community. The focus is on the transcendent. The people together join in acknowledging *who* is God, and by that same token recognize their own limits and dependencies. The community is by the very definition of the word, a *fellowshiping* community. In its family-like shape there is the potential for intimate sharing, providing one with the security of belonging. On the basis of its fellowship the community of faith is also a *healing* community. The compassion of Christ moves its members to reach out in ministry to the sufferers in their midst. As the *ekklesia,* the people called out by the Spirit of God, the community of faith is a *witnessing* community. The concept of *vocation* or calling, inherent in this mission, provides one with a purpose—a direction—for living.

Each of these functions of the congregation is of significance to the needs of the people. We shall explore each of them in terms of its potential resource for pastoral care and counseling.

A Worshiping Community

The specific faith of the congregation is expressed and supported by liturgical and communal practices associated with worship. The people of God gather together to affirm their identity as the people of God. The gathering times are characterized by traditions, remembrances, and reenactments. We are a people with a history; we are also a people with expectations. Worship is the expression of devotion to the God in whom these roots and hopes reside.

The worship form in which these roots and hopes are united in a present realization of intimacy is the sacrament of the Holy Communion or the Lord's Supper or the Eucharist—depending upon the description of the sacrament one wishes to emphasize. It is the most ecumenical of worship forms, although some denominations reject the label of sacrament, preferring instead the word *rite.* This sacrament or rite will serve as our illustration of the worshiping community as a resource for pastoral care and counseling.

The Holy Communion is a drama in which the participants reenact the original meal in the upper room. They are involved in a happening. The communication is basically through nonverbal symbols. The verbal accompaniment in the words of

institution of the sacrament labels the meaning of the participants' nonverbal activities. The Lord's Supper is a sacrament
of reconciliation. It has been called the visible Word because
of its dramatic portrayal of the Good News. Christ is the host
of his Supper. The food and drink that are served and received
are the elements of his reconciliation, namely, his body and
blood as symbolized or conveyed in the bread and wine. This
union of elements in nature, bread and wine, with the elements of redemption, body and blood, is a continuation at the
cultic level of the union of the human with the divine in the
person of Christ. In partaking of the one loaf and the one cup,
individuals form one body. The sacrament also has a future
orientation. "For as often as you eat this bread and drink this
cup, you proclaim the Lord's death until he comes" (1 Cor.
11:26). "Until he comes" symbolizes the hope of the resurrection to life eternal.

The sacrament dramatizes the context of pastoral counseling.
Eduard Thurneysen defines pastoral counseling as an *extra*-
ordinary ministry, dependent for its function in the church
upon the ordinary ministries. Pastoral counseling is desired
when a person experiences a personal crisis or some less critical
concern and needs the ministry of the pastor in a more personally involved way than is possible in the ordinary ministries
of teaching, preaching, and the administration of the sacrament. Yet, by its definition, it is a ministry associated with a
worshiping community. In the sacrament the reconciling
power which is at the heart of pastoral counseling is dramati-
cally symbolized, and the pastor who counsels is the pastor
who is ordained as the administrator of this sacrament.

Lay people, of course, also do pastoral care and counseling.
In fact lay people *must* do pastoral care and counseling since
the need is too great to be allotted solely to the clergy and since
the membership of the church as the body of Christ is composed of interdependent members who minister to one another.
The priesthood of the believer has its other side of the coin in

the *pastorhood* of the believer. Ordination for a task does not exclude lay people from involvement in that task, but rather describes what is meant by the ministry of the church.

An important element in worship is the offering of praise and thanksgiving to God. From its earliest celebration the Sacrament was called the Eucharist (thanksgiving) because it was the occasion for such thanksgiving. The act of receiving in the sacrament is joined with the response of the receiver. The prominence of thanksgiving in the participation in the Eucharist is an encouragement to the participants to join in this expression of gratitude. Praising God is one of the healthiest of all human activities.

As the Lord's Supper, the eating and drinking together in the sacrament is a symbol of family intimacy. The "taking within" of the elements of reconciliation as a corporate activity symbolizes the removal of barriers to intimacy. The divisive "wall of partition" has been taken away by an act of atonement. The low self-image is confronted by a love that is unconditional. This tangible assurance of divine acceptance is offered to the participants as individuals and as a body.

Participating in the Supper is an expression of the deepest kind of intimate experience. In what is considered by many as a Johannine reference to the Lord's Supper, Jesus is reported as saying, "He who eats my flesh and drinks my blood remains in me, and I in him" (John 6:56). Such imagery describes an internalized union—"the Spirit himself bearing witness with our spirit" (Rom. 8:16) that we are his. Through the palpable bread and wine the impalpable communion with Christ takes place. The transcendent Lord is immanently present. I am acquainted with a church where the Communion inscription on the altar is not the familiar, "take and eat," but rather "taste and see." The emphasis is on knowing through sensory experience. The incarnational character of God's revelation in Christ is continued in the sacrament.

The communion with Christ in the Supper is through the

elements of reconciliation. "The cup of blessing which we bless; is it not a participation in the blood of Christ? The bread which we break, is it not a participation in the body of Christ?" (1 Cor. 10:16). It is also through one's fellow participants. The *head* of the body is known only in conjunction with the rest of the body. We discern Christ's body not only in the bread, but also in the participants. The Lord is taken in and shared. The role of the symbol in the sacrament is to communicate that which it symbolizes. The walls that alienate break down as spectators become participants, and individuals become members one of another.

The act of eating and drinking with one another at the table of the Lord is an expression of the common enjoyment of life. Through physical sensation and social intimacy the sensuous and the spiritual are integrated in the worship experience. Bread and wine are tasted, and the body of believers is visible. In the context of communion with the Creator, the participants celebrate their common enjoyment of his creation.

Yet the tragic dimension is also present. The bread and wine are his broken body and shed blood. The positive affirmation through remembrance and reenactment is without illusions: the creation that is enjoyed is also the creation under judgment and in need of redemption. As often as we eat the bread and drink the cup, we proclaim the Lord's *death* until he comes (2 Cor. 11:26). The celebration in the sacrament is an affirmation that creation has been redeemed. He who died also is risen. Redemption is not simply a past event, but also a process in the present that looks to the future for completion. He who died and is risen is also he who will come again.

The Lord's Supper is in the shape of a family meal. Jesus instituted it in the circle of his own intimates, his disciples, at the family-oriented Passover celebration. The family meal is traditionally a time of intimate communion, a time of sharing of experiences. "Let me tell you about my day" someone says, and soon others are telling about theirs. The worshiping community is concomitant with the fellowshiping community.

The Fellowshiping Community

The congregation as a fellowshiping community provides a sense of belonging—a support group in time of stress. In a day when we speak nostalgically about extended families, the congregation provides an extended family in our midst. When parents bring their children to the church for baptism or dedication, they are witnessing to the role of the congregation as their larger family. Those churches that look upon baptism as a sacrament, in which the child is covenanted to God through the reception of his unconditional love as this is symbolized or conveyed by the tangible application of water, also look upon the congregation before whom the child is baptized as the community which receives the child into its fellowship and care. While I do not wish to imply that the dedication of children in churches that do not baptize infants is tantamount to baptism, I am assuming that the congregation in whose presence the child is dedicated plays a similar role of extended family for the child and its parents.

Families in isolation cannot be for their members what each of them needs for their healthy development. The nuclear family of mother, father, and children is subjected to too many overpowering cultural and societal influences to function autonomously, particularly in our day of rapid social change in values and priorities. Parents need the congregation—the parish—to assist in the nurture of their children. They also are needed by the congregation, where they can relate to children other than their own, as well as to other parents, as they contribute to the support system of the larger family. Children and youth, in turn, can relate to other adults than their parents, as well as to other youth and children.

Marriages also need the extended family of the congregation

for their support and development. It is rare when one's personal and social needs can be met solely within the marital relationship. Like individuals, married couples need to belong to a larger fellowship for their own growth, as well as that of the marriage. During premarital guidance the pastor has the opportunity to inquire into a couple's potential relationship with a congregation, and to emphasize the value to their marriage of this particular kind of extended family. "The church," says Henri Nouwen in *Reaching Out,* "is perhaps one of the few places left where we can meet people who are different than we are, but with whom we can form a larger family." The single, the married, those living alone and those living with others, all need the larger community to satisfy what Abraham Maslow calls "the belongingness need."

As a community of faith the congregation offers more than human togetherness and effective support systems. As Nouwen describes it, "The Christian community is not a closed circle of people embracing each other, but a forward-moving group of companions bound together by the same voice asking for their attention." As an extended family bound together by this transcendant voice, what the congregation offers in common is more important than other differences. The fellowship of the community centers around this transcendent dimension with its traditions, festivals, ceremonies, and celebrations which are associated also with worship. While we distinguish the fellowshiping community from the worshiping community for descriptive purposes, it cannot be separated from it.

This community not only receives those who enter into its midst, but also takes the initiative to reach out to those who need encouragement to enter. The model that is followed is that of the Good Shepherd. Though 99 of the 100 sheep are safely in the fold, the shepherd leaves these to go into the dark to seek the one that is lost. Many congregations also provide the opportunity for fellowship in smaller groups in which persons with particular needs or in specific situations can give and receive in mutual sharing. Others have "growth groups" whose purpose is to minister to one another—usually through study programs—in developing one's potential under God. It is through such groups that the pastor may initiate a counselee into the fellowship. The fellowshiping community is also a healing community.

The Healing Community

Wesley Methodist Church is a downtown church in Minneapolis whose membership literally is dying. The pastor, John Oman, found himself ministering more in bereavement than in anything else. At the same time his congregation was composed of many widows and widowers. When it occurred to him that he had a rich pastoral resource within the congregation for his ministry, he invited these widowed people to meet with him to plan a lay ministry to the bereaved. For the past 15 years the result is a supplemental lay ministry in the pastoral care of the bereaved that has outlived Oman's pastorate. Each year there is a training period of six weeks for new recruits to this ministry. When someone dies, the pastor selects a grief minister from his group and introduces him or her to the bereaved. This grief minister commits him or herself to minister to the bereaved person or family for a year, making regular contacts that complement the pastor's ministry.

The grief ministry at Wesley Church is one example of the lay pastorate in the congregation. It is a pastoral administrative challenge to organize this potential so that the congregation is in reality a healing community. Training programs in lay pastoral care are a vital part of this administrative task. Selected people can be solicited, educated, and assigned to complementing ministries under the pastor's direct or delegated supervision.

In Bethel Lutheran Church of Northfield, Minnesota, a small-town parish, the pastor, Ronald Golberg, instituted a *lay discipleship program* with a double purpose: to assist people in their spiritual growth and to equip them to minister to those who need their help. Although the program began only three years ago, three groups have been through it. The core curriculum, besides including Bible and doctrine and spiritual growth, focuses on lay counseling. Role-play is a frequent method, with a person other than the participants serving as observer-evaluator. The "lay disciples" may be "general practitioners" or may specialize in problem areas such as parenthood, marriage, divorce, and money management. Golberg sums up the program: "Our members have their Ph.D.'s in *life,* and the church needs to recognize that."

Those in the congregation who have been through their own ordeals and have come to some sort of resolution or way of coping with them are usually the most helpful to others who are in the midst of similar traumas. In my own family's bereavement over the death of our oldest daughter, for example, we found this particular kind of support tremendously comforting. On one occasion when my grief was most acute, I called a friend whom I had not seen or heard from in seven years. I wanted to talk with him because I had been with him in his grief after two of his children were killed in a motorcycle accident. Shortly after this we had moved from the community. I now felt as he did then. The question I wanted to ask him was, "How long does the pain last?" I knew he would have "inside" information on that. As I had anticipated, it turned out to be a most helpful call.

Those who have been through similar traumas are not threatened by the brokenness of those who are suffering. They understand the pain and the questions and the protests—and accept them. They even anticipate them and help the sufferers to prepare for the continuing ordeal.

Utilizing people who have endured suffering to help those now in similar straits, is an expansion of the Alcoholics Anonymous format, which to date has been our most effective approach to those afflicted with alcoholism. The sober alcoholic knows how to approach another alcoholic, understanding not only the pain but also the defense system that is an obstacle to overcoming the problem. The specific groups in churches in which those with similar needs support each other are also an adaptation of the AA meeting in which alcoholics reenforce each other for sobriety as they "turn [their] will and [their] lives over to the care of God as [they] understand him."

But compassionate and understanding people are helpful as care-givers regardless of what they have or have not experienced. Compassion and understanding are qualities that are nurtured by our exposure to the Spirit of Christ, through the fellowship of believers. Consequently one should be able to discover such people in the congregation and use them in the healing community.

Such a program is also an opportunity for the pastor's counselees. Since they have been receivers, they too need to give. When the pastor senses that the time is right—when the person, or couple, or family's recovery is sufficiently stable—he or she can ask them to join in the training program for lay ministry. Again, it is significant to note the comparison with chemical-addiction training centers in which a good portion of the counselors are former users. As counselees join in giving to others what they have received, they continue to receive healing themselves. We receive as we give. I have known people who seemed locked into perpetual bereavement over the loss of a loved one who regained their interest in life by entering into some form of ministry to others. But they all needed help to get started. A pastor can say to such a person, "Look, I'm ministering to Mrs. Smith who seems overwhelmed by an ordeal that you know much about. I need your help. May I arrange an appointment for you with Mrs. Smith, so that you can talk with her. She needs you—and so do I."

If the person heeds the request, the pastor may have assisted in the rehabilitation of a battle-wounded veteran. At the same time he or she is receiving valuable help in ministry. A sufferer can enter too soon into the ministering role—before the wounds have had sufficient time in the healing process. One can also stay out too long, when the necessary withdrawal for healing threatens to become a way of life.

We can scarcely discuss the congregation as a healing community without facing the glaring contradiction to all that has been said—the horror stories about the destructive activities of this or that congregation. As extended families, congregations often act like other families. Those who love each other may at times also hate each other. Those who speak with affection may at other times speak with contempt. Such seems to be the nature of intimate relationships. Nor was it necessarily any better in our pristine past. The biblical church of Corinth, for example, was scandalized by the behavior of its members at their celebration of the Lord's Supper. Family meals are potentially times of intimacy. By that same token they are potentially also times of strife. In this instance the strife was so severe that the missionary who had founded the church felt constrained to intervene by letter. The clash was between the haves and the have-nots, and it had turned the *agape* feast in which the sacrament was then celebrated into a brawl. Yet because of it, we have in Paul's letter of intervention our oldest and most explicit description of the Lord's Supper.

Division within congregations continues to be an embarrassment. Yet congregations exist in a fallen world and are composed of sinners. We need to begin with this reality before we can effect any change for the better. Nothing is changed by denying reality. Yet despite the unpleasant realities, the potential is still inherent in every congregation to move in the direction of a healing community. This potential centers in the resources for healing that belong to the congregation—the faith we have in Christ, the reconciling love of God, the Scripture, the sacraments, prayer and meditation, and the mission of

God's people. If you are pastor of a congregation that is more divisive than healing, begin with those who are ready to move. Inspire them with the vision of the healing community, and educate them in this ministry, and let them take it from there. Nouwen says it well: "As long as we are willing to face the contrast [between the real and the ideal] and struggle to minimize it, the tension can keep us humble by allowing us to offer our service to others without being whole ourselves." This applies also to the pastor who can feel as unworthy as his or her congregation of being an instrument of God's healing.

Colonial Edina Church, a large suburban Congregational church in my area has a support group program that has mushroomed since it began just four years ago. It began as a weekly group for "hurting women," where these women could talk things over with a pastoral counselor and with other women. The program now also includes an evening support group for men and women, a job transition support group, and a grief support group. Approximately 70 people receive pastoral care through these groups in one week with only six to eight hours of pastoral-staff time. As the minister of pastoral counseling, David Williamson says, the support groups are both "very efficient and very effective." Leadership of the groups is in the hands of laypersons who themselves have been equipped by the training programs of the church. These groups extend the pastoral care and counseling ministry of the congregation to more people and over a longer period of time than is usually feasible in a one-to-one pastoral relationship.

Even our fractured and broken groups can be healing. Perfection is only a goal—not an attainment—for both pastor and congregation. The congregation, like the individual believer, imperfect, flawed, distorted, and sinful, is justified by grace through faith. Counselees who have been through this same route of acceptance are able to accept and profit from a group that owes its identity to the forgiveness of sin.

The Witnessing Community

The community of faith is a community with a calling—a mission. Those who believe in Christ are called to follow him. Those who receive the light are obligated to reflect it. The members of Christ's body are also his disciples. When Matthias was chosen to replace the deceased Judas, he was described as a "witness to his resurrection" (Acts 1:22). It was the function of the community of faith to witness to its faith. The word to witness, *martyreo,* is the root for our English word *martyr,* indicating the risk involved in being a witness.

Although the original description of the disciples' witness concerns the resurrection, the witness is to all that God has revealed to us through Christ. The mission of the community is to reach out as a leaven in society with the gospel of reconciliation. This may mean ministering in a priestly way to individuals, as has been described in the healing ministry. It may also mean witnessing in a prophetic way in regard to the social structures of society which may be unjust or even oppressive to certain people. As a community, the congregation has the people-power to change these structures. Because it is difficult to obtain unanimity on the use of its people-power, paracongregations of like minded disciples are more likely to be the operating model.

The Christian's calling is also expressed in one's occupation. People cannot, nor should they, all go the route of the ordained ministry to fulfill this calling. So what is the potential in their present occupation for living out their witness? Some have seemingly more important tasks than others so far as shaping the way we live together in society. Congregations often have people in positions of influence in society. Their sense of purpose in these positions could be enhanced if they saw them as ways of fulfilling their calling as disciples. But all jobs or functions—from the nonskilled laborer to the judge on the bench—make a contribution to the life of the community.

How then can we see the relationship between our vocation and our occupation? This is a function of the congregation as a worshiping community, in the preaching and teaching of the Word. Yet seeing the relationship and responding to it may be two different things. For the latter, one may need courage as well as knowledge, since one's witness to justice and compassion may not always be appreciated. But if one has a support group in the congregation in which the members reenforce each other in their calling as God's people in their jobs and support each other when the "going gets tough," one may make different decisions in the job than were one alone and frightened. Without the reenforcement from the body of Christ one may begin to think according to the institutional model within which one works and lose the tension with the values associated with the way of Christ. The Metropolitan Associates of Philadelphia have published a manual entitled, *A Strategy of Hope,* for the organization and functioning of such support groups in a congregation, the essential feature of which is this mutual strengthening of one another during conflicts in one's work where the concern for honesty and justice is controversial. (Kenneth Vernon, ed., 101 S. 13th St., Philadelphia, Pa., 1972.)

While there may be a risk to being a witness, the other side of the coin is that it is this witness that gives meaning and purpose to our lives. The congregation, therefore, provides a resource for pastoral care and counseling by helping people to discover this purpose for their lives by giving them opportunities to serve as disciples of Christ. As Frankl has emphasized, people need meaning for their lives if they are to function as human beings. While we bring our sense of meaning to our actions, these actions in turn are necessary for the expression of this meaning. Without them our sense of purpose and even of worth, is frustrated. "People are sick" says Tillich, "not only because they have not received love but because they are not allowed to give love." The witnessing community has, by its definition, a mission that involves all of its members. Those who have received need also to give. The nature of Christ's self-giving is a call to our own. "The disciple is not above his teacher" (Matt. 10:24). We are "not our own," since we have been "bought with a price"; "the costly grace" of God's gift of forgiveness moves us to live for more than ourselves (1 Cor. 6:19-20).

Again, we need to face the contrast that too often occurs between what should be and what is. The activities that some congregations engage in may bear little resemblance to their witness. Congregations can conceive of their purpose more in terms of what other organizations and institutions are doing rather than in their unique calling. As a people united by a common calling the congregation, as well as its clergy, needs to ask how the activities to which they are devoting their energies are related to this calling.

The activities of the church, however, need not be directly related to service projects or societal concerns to be related to the witness. The fact that the community of faith is not just for each other, but also for God can influence how we understand our particular contributions within it. Even the building where the congregation gathers is more than a building: it is a sanctuary, a house of God. Some may find their major contribution in the maintenance and in the beautification of this building and its grounds. Whether it is through contributing of ourselves to the congregation as a community of faith or through our occupations or other functions in society, our calling is expressed in doing whatever we do "as serving the Lord" (Col. 3:23).

Interrelationship of Ministries

If I were a counselor in another helping profession, I believe I would envy the pastoral counselor the resources he or she has in the congregation as a community of faith. As Howard Clinebell puts it, "No other helping profession has a comparable supportive fellowship available year-in, year-out, to undergird its work." Without minimizing the value of the one-to-one relationship or of group counseling, each of these is tremendously enhanced when it is carried on within the context of the congregation. The congregation provides the pastor with other ministering contacts with his or her counselees, provided, of course, that they are involved in the same congregation. His or her preaching, leadership in worship, teaching, administration, and group-oriented ministries all tend to be mutually reenforcing with the counseling ministry. The pastor's proficiency in each of these ministries is increased by his or her involvement in the others.

In *How to Start Counseling* (Abingdon Press, 1955) my emphasis was on how preaching, calling, and administration each has a mutual relationship to pastoral care and counseling. Preaching, for example, while not adapted, as is counseling, to minister to the more serious and deep-rooted problems of people, is both a preventative of problems and an introduction to the counselor and what he has to offer. The counseling ministry, in turn, provides the pastor with insights for his sermons, since people with serious problems are experiencing in a greater degree the frustrations and conflicts others may be experiencing. Naturally, he or she must not use counseling cases as illustrations since maintaining confidences is of utmost priority. Counseling, nevertheless, keeps the pastor alert to where his or her people are in their daily battles with "quiet desperation." Counselees, in turn, seem to receive much from the sermons of the pastor with whom they are counseling. They may even bring up the sermon in their counseling session to express what it said to them. A similar mutuality exists within the teaching ministry. We have referred previously to the interrelationship with the administrative and worship leadership ministries.

Each of these other ministries of the pastor is also a preventative ministry. They are nurturing ministries and therefore contributors to the health of the congregation. These are the *ordinary* ministries which are assisted in their limits by the *extra*ordinary ministries of pastoral care and counseling. As pastor and people work together at the task of enhancing the ordinary and nurturing ministries of the congregation, the ministries of pastoral care and counseling will have a strong and supportive base from which to function.

Summary

The congregation provides many resource opportunities for pastoral care and counseling. In the worship-oriented sacrament of Holy Communion, these opportunities are all symbolized in this drama of participation. The uniqueness of the community in its transcendent orientation is expressed through its worship, fellowship, and mission, each of which constitutes a therapeutic activity. The pastor is a catalyst for this ministry of the congregation within its own membership as well as beyond it. The tangible support of the people of God can be the decisive element in a person's recovery from the traumas of life. Those who have endured these traumas and crises are potential counselors for those in the midst of them.

The criteria for the pastoral use of the community of faith, as with other resources, focus on the pastor's assessment of ways in which his care of a person could be supplemented by an involvement in the life of the congregation, as well as the person's readiness for any particular congregational activity. Since pastoral care and counseling are a part, rather than the whole, of the pastoral ministry, the pastor is professionally justified in his or her encouraging a counselee's involvement in the total program of ministry. How this involvement comes about is influenced by many other factors. The congregation's own reaching out to the counselee is one of these. The pastor's referral of the counselee to specific opportunities in the life of the congregation is another. The counselee is also a potential participant in the lay ministry of the congregation. This involvement, of course, depends on the pastor and counselee's determination that the counselee's progress has been sufficiently stabilized to assume this responsibility.

Epilogue

We have explored the uniqueness of pastoral care and counseling among their fellow disciplines in the helping professions. We have seen that this uniqueness is based on the specific faith of the Christian tradition that undergirds and shapes these ministries. Pastoral care and counseling function within a system other than the usual dyad between counselor and counselee, or the interrelationships between counselor and couple, family, or other groupings. In the perspective of pastoral care and counseling, each participant has at least a *potential* relationship with God, and this relationship is an acknowledged and functional contributor to the processes of these ministries. Implicitly or explicitly, depending on the context of each particular system, this expansion of the usual therapeutic system is a dynamic quality within pastoral care and counseling.

Pastors have something unique and helpful to offer to people who are hurting. Consequently, they need to be as skilled and comfortable in the use of these distinctly religious resources in their counseling as they are frequently becoming with the language, concepts, and tools of psychology and psychotherapy. Other professionals have observed on occasion that pastors are hesitant in the very area of their distinct identity. Menninger Clinic psychologist Paul Pruyser comments in *Minister as*

Diagnostician that pastors "seem to like psychological language better than theological language." His conclusion: "It is a jarring note when any professional person no longer knows what his basic science is, or finds no use for it." A psychiatrist friend of mine who also works with pastors in clinical pastoral education comments that pastors seem almost embarrassed to use their own God-talk symbols.

People who seek pastoral care and counseling may be disappointed when they encounter this reluctance on the part of the pastor to focus on the religious area. As Pruyser puts it, "How disappointing, then, when his pastor quickly translates his quest into psychological or social terms." I have talked to people who have expressed precisely this same disappointment with their experience in pastoral counseling.

It may be helpful for pastors to bear in mind that people who seek our ministry may *not* be using their religion as a defense against facing their real problems and responsibilities. (Psychological terms can also be used in this defensive manner.) In contrast these people are more likely to have chosen *pastoral* counseling because they *want* to confront their problems and sense that the theological route is the most *direct* way for them to do this. They may feel "at home" with the particular anthropology of the Christian tradition in which the human being is viewed as a creature in need of harmony with the Creator. The hesitance of some pastors to affirm their own professional identity—in addition to the fact that some pastors also misuse this identity—may reflect the longstanding sense of inferiority which pastors experience when they work with or compare themselves to other helping professionals. Although many pastors have overcome this inferiority and are at ease with other professionals as *persons,* the inferiority may be manifesting itself now in a reluctance to affirm their uniqueness as *professionals.*

It is my hope that this book will contribute to this affirmation of a distinct pastoral identity. I hope also that it will stimulate others to do further research into these ministerial resources of the Christian tradition. The awareness of our identity will in itself enhance this identity as we grow in our appreciation of our professional roots. These roots are also our heritage. Our theological tradition characterizes our ministry.

This context for ministry is open-minded in its development, as practice feeds back into knowledge, and knowledge leads again to practice. Each pastor is part of this developmental process as he or she works collegially with peers in the pursuit of professional growth. This collegiality needs also at times to be extended to the other helping professionals to provide a complementary dialogue within which our distinctly pastoral identity is clarified. Because an interprofessional team is by its very nature complementary, it contains the potential for mutual referral.

This developmental process also needs to include at times the lay persons of our congregations who have been equipped by their pastors, as well as by other lay persons, to minister to each other within the community of faith and beyond it, a mutuality of ministry which includes also the pastor and his or her family. In this pastoral collegiality within the congregation much can be learned and consequently added to our evolving knowledge of pastoral care and counseling.

Bibliography

Basic Types of Pastoral Counseling, Howard Clinebell. Nashville: Abingdon, 1966.

The incorporation of a variety of counseling approaches into the perspective and practice of the Christian ministry.

Biblical Themes for Pastoral Care, William B. Oglesby. Nashville: Abingdon, 1980.

A study with *verbatim* examples of the role of the Bible in pastoral care in terms of specific biblical themes, dialectically presented, that are implicit in the pastoral dialogue.

The Integration of Theology and Psychology, Bruce Narramore and John D. Carter. Grand Rapids: Zondervan, 1979.

An analysis and evaluation of current attempts to relate the resources of psychology to the pastoral ministries of the church.

Kerygma and Counseling, Thomas Oden. Philadelphia: Westminster, 1966.

A demonstration of the similarities between the human self-disclosure therapy of Carl Rogers and the divine self-disclosure theology of Karl Barth.

The Minister as Crisis Counselor, David Switzer. New York: Abingdon, 1974.

A description of the dynamics of crises—grief, divorce, and other family traumas—and of the pastor's role and function as a crisis counselor.

The Minister as Diagnostician, Paul Pruyser. Philadelphia: Westminster, 1976.

A clinical psychologist's suggestion of categories for diagnosing personal disturbances based on the particularity of the pastoral ministry as a theologically-oriented discipline.

The Minister and the Care of Souls, Daniel Day Williams. New York: Harper, 1961; reprint, 1977.

A reflection on the theological and religious issues inherent in pastoral care as it relates to the office of the ministry and to the church as a worshiping community.

The Moral Context of Pastoral Care, Don S. Browning. Philadelphia: Westminster, 1976.

A series of lectures on the need to restore to pastoral care the dialectic of Law-Gospel and the Judeo-Christian methodologies for the cultivation of the religious life.

Parish Counseling, Edgar Jackson. New York: Aronson, 1975.

A veteran parish pastor's presentation and analysis of pastoral counseling cases occurring within the context of the parish ministry.

Pastoral Counseling, Wayne Oates. Philadelphia: Westminster, 1974.

A description of the particular tensions inherent in the nature of pastoral counseling as a professional ministry of the church.

Pastoral Counseling Guidebook, Charles Kemp. Nashville: Abingdon, 1971.

A condensed digest in modified outline form of every conceivable aspect of pastoral counseling including a comprehensive bibliography in each area of pastoral care.

Preface to Pastoral Theology, Seward Hiltner. New York: Abingdon, 1958.

A definitive work on the distinctiveness of pastoral theology among the theological disciplines.

The Promise of Counseling, C. W. Brister. New York: Harper and Row, 1978.

An investigation into the potentials for healing through pastoral counseling and of specific pastoral approaches that may facilitate the actualization of these potentials.

Theology and Pastoral Care, John Cobb. Philadelphia: Fortress, 1977.

A description, both theoretical and applied, of pastoral care and counseling in the light of process theology.

Theology and Pastoral Counseling, Edward E. Thorton. Philadelphia, Fortress, 1964.

A description via verbatim case material of the interpenetration of pastoral care and counseling with pastoral theology in which the author's own pilgrimage as a pastoral theologian helps him to perceive the dialectical relationship between health and salvation.

The Wounded Healer, Henri Nouwen. Garden City: Doubleday, 1975.

A sensitive approach to the intrapersonal and interpersonal dynamics of the pastoral relationship in its openness to the Spirit of God.